AN INSTINCT
FOR DRAGONS

DAVID E. JONES

D1546348

ROUTLEDGE
NEW YORK LONDON

Published in 2002 by
Routledge
29 West 35th Street
New York, NY 10001

Published in Great Britain by
Routledge
11 New Fetter Lane
London EC4P 4EE

First Routledge paperback edition, 2002.
Printed in the United States of America on acid-free paper.

10 9 8 7 6 5 4 3 2 1

Library of Congress Cataloging-in-Publication Data

Jones, David E., 1942-
An instinct for dragons / by David E. Jones
p. cm.
Includes bibliographical references (p.) and index.
ISBN 0-415-92721-8—0-415-93729-9 (pbk.)
1. Dragons. 2. Genetic psychology. I. Title

GR830.D7 /j65 2000

398'.469-dc21   99-462234

CONTENTS

ACKNOWLEDGMENTS

I wish to thank my wife, Jane, for her major editorial assistance and encouragement. My colleague Professor Ronald L. Wallace of the University of Central Florida offered invaluable critique on the sections dealing with biocultural theory, while physical anthropologist Trenton Holiday of Tulane University reviewed my discussion of human evolution. Thanks also go to Christopher Savage and Lucus Johnson for the original illustrations. Of course, the final responsibility for the resulting product must be mine.

INTRODUCTION

From the shadows of an oak grove on a distant ridge, it watched the humans move from chore to chore—feeding animals, hoeing a small garden, pulling stumps from a rocky field. A faint curl of smoke rose from the chimney of the tidy thatched cottage. A child laughed behind the barn as she played with her new kitten, and window-box flowers nodded in the gentle spring breeze.

Groaning like a furnace, it hoisted its reptilian body from the ground, labored into the air on stunted wings, and rolled, belching sulphurous smoke, like a churning thundercloud toward the small farm. Its hideous roar shattered the morning calm, announcing the presence of the most terrible of creatures. The humans ran for their lives.

What creature does your imagination conjure? Can you name it? People everywhere have been able to. They have had a mental category for the creature that has been called "the oldest, the first, the most basic monster" (McHargue 1988, 27) as well as "the most venerable symbol employed in ornamental art and the favorite and most highly decorated motif in artistic design . . . the inspiration of much, if not most, of the world's great literature in every age and clime, and the nucleus around which a wealth of ethical symbolism has accumulated throughout the ages" (Smith 1919, 77).

The Chinese call it *lung;* the Hawaiians, *kelekona* or perhaps *mo'o.* It is *zmaj* to Croatians and Serbians, *lohikaarme* to the Finns, and *unktena* to the Cherokee Indians of North America. The Polish tell of *smok,* the Turks of the *ejderha,* the Maori of New Zealand of the *tarakona,* and the Hungarians of *sarkany.* The Japanese say *tatsu,* the Welsh *draig,* the Ger-

FIGURE 1: A CLASSICAL WESTERN DRAGON WITH THE TALONED FEET, WINGS, SCALES, HORNS, AND FIERY BREATH TYPICAL OF MOST OF THE WORLD'S DRAGONS.

mans *lindwurm,* the Dutch *draak,* and the Lakota Sioux *unhcegila.* The creature is named in Aztec, Arabic, Danish, Estonian, Finnish, Greek, Hebrew, Icelandic, Rumanian, Russian, Turkish, and others. English speakers call it *dragon* (fig. 1).

Most peoples at some point in their history have believed that the dragon was real. Prior to the sixteenth century, thousands of eyewitness accounts of dragon sightings were recorded. In the British Isles alone, from the eleventh to the thirteenth centuries, the following towns reported encounters with dragons: Dornoch, Ben Vair, Kirkton, Anwick, Wantley, Penmynnedd, Denbigh, Bromfield, Brinsop, Llanrhaedr-Ym-Mochant, Deerhurst, Uffington, Ludham, St. Osyth, Bures, St. Leonard's Forest, Bisterne, Aler, Kingston St. Mary, Churchstanton, Carhmaptin, Exe Valley, and Helston (Dickinson 1979, 74–75).

The source of the dragon, however, is a mystery. How can something so impossible exist in the art, mythology, religion, and legend of so many places? Let us begin by removing one of the most obvious parallels, the dinosaurs. They cannot model for the dragon, because dinosaurs had become extinct many millions of years before the evolution of humans. Some writers, however, have proposed that it may have been not the experience of real dinosaurs that prompted the appearance of the dragon myth, but rather the misidentification of the fossilized remains of ancient dinosaurs. Of course, the hoary epistemological question rears its head: How can one recognize something as a dragon unless one already knows what a dragon is? The dragon image is perforce prior to the fossil identification.

Other researchers grappling with the dragon puzzle suggest that the dragon of world mythology came from primal man's experience with real creatures. For example, on five small Indonesian islands in the Lesser Sunda group, a type of monitor lizard popularly known as the Komodo dragon stalks the thickets, taking down animals as large as deer, wild pigs, and occasionally people. Then there are the giants of the python family. Some, like the rock python and the Indian python, reach a length of almost thirty feet and a weight of several hundred muscular pounds. These creatures have been around longer than humans, and early contact with big pythons at a time when protohumans were substantially smaller than humans today was no doubt traumatic.

The flaw in the hypothesis that the dragon is derived from ancient encounters with various kinds of carnivores and large reptiles rests in the fact that the dragon is universal, while the above-mentioned animals are not. Most of them, in fact, come from tiny isolated corners of the earth.

The dragon puzzle persists. There seems to be no physically based theory to explain why the dragon populates the imagination of peoples in seemingly all cultures. What, after all, is this beast that all the world knows—this creature that never was?

My interest in the dragon problem was ignited one day while I was preparing notes for an undergraduate lecture on primate behavior. To provide an example, I selected the African vervet, a monkey undistinguished for the most part except for one fascinating aspect of its behavior. The vervets give distinctive alarm calls at the appearance of three different predators: leopards, martial eagles, and pythons. Further, each of these calls stimulates responses directly related to escaping the predator (Struhsaker 1967). When the vervets are on the ground and hear the leopard call, the troop quickly climbs into the trees. The monkeys position themselves on the tips of the smallest branches, which will give no support to a prowling leopard. When the eagle alarm call is sounded, the vervets automatically look skyward. If on the ground, they run into the bushes; if in the trees, they immediately drop to the ground to avoid the swooping attack of the eagle. Snake alarms, on the other hand, cause the vervets to look down, often from a bipedal standing posture to gain a better view of the ground.

After completing my notes for the vervet lecture, I was absent-mindedly gathering the books I had used when one fell open to a page headed "The Vervets' Predators." Images of an eagle, a leopard, and a snake were featured. Suddenly, in my mind's eye, the three predator images merged. The leopard body took on the outer look of the python, resulting in a large reptilian body with four clawed feet and a mouth full of sharp teeth. When the wings of the martial eagle attached to the shoulders of the blended leopard/python, I saw a dragon! (fig. 2)

This unsought insight focused my attention on dragons. I found them everywhere. Actress Sigourney Weaver, a classic dragon slayer—pure of heart and defender of the weak—has descended four times, as of last count, into the dank caverns of the *Alien* beast. J. R. R. Tolkien's treasure-

Figure 2: THREE PREDATORS WHO MOST THREATENED OUR ANCES-
TORS—THE EAGLE, THE LEOPARD, AND THE SNAKE—MERGE IN
MYTHOLOGY TO BECOME A SINGLE CREATURE, THE DRAGON.

hoarding dragon Smaug looks down from my *Hobbit* calendar. Somewhere, thousands of teenage boys are playing Dungeons and Dragons, while their parents listen to a CD of Wagner's *Der Ring des Nibelungen,* a musical tale featuring Fafnir, a dragon. On the Internet dozens, if not hundreds, of dragon sites throb with life, and around the world the dragon's potent name and image are widely employed by sports teams.

Further, sightings of creatures that would have readily been considered dragons not that many years ago continue unabated to the present day. Most have heard of the Loch Ness monster. A similar creature is reported by the people living beside Lake Seljordsvatnet in Norway. In fact, reptilian lake monsters are known from Japan to the Great Lakes of the United States and Canada. These instances of the dragon in modern life are reminders that tales of the dragon are not merely fascinations reserved for children and ancient nonliterate peoples. It may be that more images of dragons exist in our skeptical society's contemporary art, lore, and cinema than ever existed among the ancients who embraced the dragon as real.

Classical Greek mythology is alive with dragons. Zeus, after defeating his father, Cronus, was confronted by Typhon, demon of the whirlwind, a beast composed of masses of coiled snakes. It had hundreds of serpent heads sprouting from its shoulders, leathery wings that darkened the sun, and a wingspan of several hundred leagues. Its eyes were said to flash fire, its roar shook the earth, and flames shot from its gaping mouth. The Greek hydra, on the other hand, was a multiheaded dragon, sometimes rendered as a giant serpent with six to nine heads and sometimes as a winged, four-footed saurian creature with a number of heads. Its breath was considered deadly. From the Egyptians, the Greeks borrowed the image of the Oroboros, the "tail eater." This dragon held its tail in its mouth and was the symbol of eternity, the "never ending." It was generally depicted as a giant winged serpent with clawed feet.

For the Romans, the Latin word *draco* identified large snakes and dragons. Perle Epstein (1973) notes of the Roman dragon, "This creature was usually represented in classical art as a fire breather with large bat's wings, a monster who spends his time in dark caves and sea grottoes guarding treasures" (34).

Dragons also populated the Scandinavian countries. Vikings raided along the European coast and the British Isles in boats with carved dragon head prows. They drew dragon images from legends that reached back to the sagas of the warrior gods. It is there that Jormungander, the Midgard Serpent, an immense serpent with a dragon's head, appears.

Folklorist Jonathan D. Evans, in his study (1984) of three dozen dragon tales in Old English and Old Norse, concludes that dragons share many common features: "The dragon's body is generally very large, serpentine, equipped with lashing tail, sharp talons, a gaping mouth with sharp teeth. Where psychological phenomena are attributed to the dragon, they are of a singularly bestial malevolence. The dragon's habitat . . . is remote and solitary. The dragon's behavioral characteristics include maleficent marauding, fire-breathing, taking of live captives, and jealous hoarding of treasure" (95).

Europe also claimed the double-headed serpent, or amphisbaena, as well as the griffin, which like the amphisbaena is an ancient type of dragon with a long history in the Mediterranean region and Near East. Its likeness varied between a composite of a lion and an eagle and that of a reptile/feline/ raptor beast, or griffin-dragon.

Asian dragons are associated with rain, soil fecundity, rivers, oceans, and floods. The worst floods were generally ascribed to a dragon's reaction to some sort of untoward mortal behavior. References to dragons are found in the earliest Chinese literature, dating to 2700 B.C. Very recognizable dragons appear during the Shang period (1600–1100 B.C.) as snake-bodied creatures with the requisite scales, claws, and a mouth full of teeth. The Chinese dragon is often depicted with spines or crests emanating from its back (fig. 3).

The dragon appears full-blown in the *Kojiki,* or "Record of Ancient Things," written in A.D. 712, the earliest Japanese account of their own history. Dipping into mythology old even at the time of the compiling of the *Kojiki,* the story tells of the storm god Susa-no-ow, a wild and footloose warrior hero and slayer of the Koshi dragon, a beast so impossibly huge that it could drape its body over eight hills and valleys at once. Trees and bushes sprouted from its scaly back, as did eight heads with blood-red eyes and eight serpentine tails.

Figure 3: THE CHINESE DRAGON, THOUGH DEPICTED AS WINGLESS IN A NUMBER OF CASES, WAS NEVERTHELESS FLIGHT-CAPABLE, AS THIS IMAGE FROM THE SHAN HAI KING INDICATES.

The Mongols tell of *leongalli,* a dragon that was half lion and half cock. The Chukchi, reindeer herders wandering the barrens of Siberia, speak in hushed tones of the worms, giant serpentlike monsters.

The subcontinent of India has a long tradition of dragon tales, and Indian religious art often depicts the creator god Vishnu reclining on the back of an enormous *naga,* or dragon-hydra. The *makara,* another type of Indian dragon, can assume a number of forms, its major manifestation being that of a creature with the tail of a snake and the head and legs of a crocodile. It also regularly appeared as a dragon or sea serpent. Heinz Mode (1973) writes of the *makara,* "nearly all are water-monsters, which occasionally develop into dragon-like four-footed creatures. This type spread from India to Kashmir, Nepal, Tibet, Indonesia and Indo-China. . . . The makara figures of South Asia can compete in number and in richness of imagination with the dragons and griffins of the western world" (140).

In a Sumerian hymn dating to 2500 B.C., we hear of Ninurta, the sun god, a large scaled creature with the forefeet of a lion and the hind feet of an eagle. And a Babylonian-Sumerian creation epic dating to about 2000 B.C. recounted the tale of Tiamat, mother of the gods, who in order to avenge the killing of her husband, transformed herself into a dragon with impervious scales, two forelegs armed with claws, a long snakelike neck and head, and a pair of horns (fig. 4). Tiamat's battalions were comprised of *sirrush,* terrifying beasts that looked part bird of prey, part serpent, part lion, and part scorpion. A very dramatic image of the *sirrush* was unearthed by German archaeologist Robert Kodeway in 1899 when he discovered the Ishtar Gate, erected by King Nebuchadnezzar II (605–562 B.C.). The *sirrush* dragon was carved with scales, a long thin tail, a neck that ended in a serpent's head, a forked tongue, and pointed horns. The front feet were those of a lion, and the back those of a raptor (fig. 5).

In Egypt, a hieroglyph of the Great God in the temple of Seti I (circa 1300 B.C.) shows a winged, snakelike creature with four clawed feet and three heads. A seal found at Susa, dating to 3000 B.C., featured a dragon with the front part an eagle and the hindpart a lion (fig. 6). In addition, the winged-serpent image is found throughout Egyptian folklore and mythology (figs. 7, 8).

Figure 4: THIS ANCIENT BABYLONIAN IMAGE OF THE DRAGON TIAMAT WAS TAKEN FROM A CYLINDER SEAL IN THE BRITISH MUSEUM.

Figure 5: THIS CLASSIC DRAGON IMAGE FROM THE ISHTAR GATE OF BABYLON WAS DISCOVERED BY ARCHAEOLOGISTS IN THE LATE NINETEENTH CENTURY.

FIGURE 6: AN ANCIENT IMAGE OF A DRAGON TAKEN FROM A CYLINDER
SEAL FOUND IN THE EXCAVATION OF SUSA SHOWS A BEAST
COMPOUNDED OF THE FOREPART OF AN EAGLE AND THE HIND
PART OF A LION.

Figure 7: WINGED SERPENT IMAGES WERE COMMON IN ANCIENT EGYPT. THIS PICTURE DEPICTS THE WINGED SERPENT OF THE GODDESS MERSOKAR.

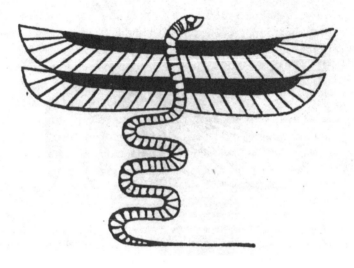

Figure 8: THE MULTIAPPENDAGED OR HYDRA EFFECT IS SEEN IN THE DOUBLE WINGS OF THE EGYPTIAN WINGED SERPENT CHANUPHIS, OR BAIT.

Two of the most famous dragon stories come from Africa. The oldest account, set in Ethiopia, tells of the rescue of Princess Andromeda and the slaying of the dragon Cetus by the Greek demigod Perseus. Cetus was described as an enormous, limbless "serpent whale" with impenetrable scales, a doglike head, a bright red crest, and two membranous wings. This type of dragon, a wyvern, is known worldwide. A second epic dragon tale is set in North Africa in the third century. This story, modeled no doubt on the earlier story of Perseus, describes the rescue from a dragon of Princess Alycone of Silene, Libya, by a young knight named George. The princess-eating dragon that the good knight killed possessed scales, a snakelike tail, four muscular legs, a powerful neck, markings on its wings that looked like eyes, and smoking vapors issuing from its mouth (fig. 9).

In west-central Africa, the Ashanti tell of a scaled beast that breathed fire from its nostrils. It was believed that its eyesight was so keen that it was able to see a fly moving miles away, and it could move along the ground so quickly that no one could catch it (Barker and Sinclair 1917, 97–101). The *mokele-mbembe,* said to look like a sauropod dinosaur, and the *inkhomi,* a crested cobra or basilisk-dragon that had a snakelike body and snake fangs plus the attributes of a rooster, have been reported for centuries by Western travelers as well as the native peoples of central Africa.

Of Oceania, Grafton Elliot-Smith (1919) noted, "We find scattered throughout the islands of the Pacific the familiar stories of the dragon" (230). A striped, two-headed snake monster lives among the Arapesh of New Guinea. It inhabits pools and caves, guards the Arapesh hunting grounds, and is particularly dangerous to childbearing women. Peoples of the traditional cultures of Samoa believed that a dragon abided as king of the gods; and the Maori, the native inhabitants of New Zealand, possess the myth of a lizard-bodied dragon as big as a whale with a huge head, a mouth full of needle-sharp teeth, four short legs, scales, claws, sharp spines across its head, and hot poisonous breath.

The aborigines of Australia speak of several types of dragons, including the Rainbow Serpent and the *bunyip;* and in Hawaii, tradition tells of the *mo-o,* a large, heavy-bodied reptile that reached a length of thirty feet more with four legs, scales, and fanglike teeth. Polynesianist Rita Knipe writes (1989) of the *mo-o,* "The lizard gods or monsters are known by several names, including Moko, or Mo'o elsewhere in Poly-

Figure 9: THIS ETHIOPIAN WINGED BIPED DRAGON WAS OF THE TYPE
CONFRONTED IN AFRICA BY THE GREEK CULTURE HERO PERSEUS
AND LATER BY THE MOST FAMOUS OF WESTERN DRAGON SLAYERS,
GEORGE OF CAPPADOCIA.

nesia, but the mythological resemblance is clear. We can best understand the primeval Mo'o as dangerous dragons" (146).

The Americas are also populated with dragons. The dragon complex raptor/serpent/cat appears in many artistic media utilized by the Inca of South America; and among the ancient high civilizations of Mesoamerica, there is a special focus on the plumed serpent, an *amphipteres* dragon. The Aztec of the Valley of Mexico knew him as Quetzalcoatl. That he was more than a green-winged snake, as his name implies, was made clear in the costuming of Aztec priests when they played his part in rituals by donning a green feathered cape and a crocodile-like mask with heavy muzzle and many sharp teeth. Between 500 B.C. and A.D. 900, the plumed serpent Kulkulkan was an important deity among the Maya of the Yucatan Peninsula.

In North America the most widely known ancient dragon image is that of the Piasa dragon (fig. 10). Its image was first described by the French priest and explorer Jacques Marquette in August 1675. While exploring the Mississippi River, he came upon several paintings eighty feet above a series of rapids and deep pools near present-day Alton, Illinois. Father Marquette described them as portraying a creature possessing horns like a deer; blood-red eyes; a body covered in scales; a tail so long that it passed entirely around its body, over its head, and between its legs; the face of a man; large, sharp teeth; the beard of a tiger; four scaly legs with taloned feet; a pair of leathery wings that spanned about seventeen feet; and smoke oozing from its nostrils. The dragon measured thirty feet in length and twelve feet in height. Many Indian tribes of the Mississippi Valley and Great Lakes regions portrayed such creatures on cliffs and rocks near dangerous rapids and deep pools.

The plumed serpent, found from the Valley of Mexico to the Great Lakes, also dwells among the Pueblo Indians of the American Southwest. The Hopi, Zuni, and Keres all honor the horned water serpent Pululukon, a creature depicted in rituals as possessing a thunderous roar, a crest of feathers, a large mouth full of sharp carnivorous teeth, and sometimes wings.

In the Northeast culture area, the Seneca Indians of New York believed in the existence of a giant horned serpent that lived in deep waters, the Doonongaes. In the Southeast, the Seminoles of Florida told of the water cougar, a composite cat/reptile that resided in deep water

Figure 10: THIS IMAGE OF THE AMERICAN DRAGON, THE PIASA, WAS RENDERED BY WILLIAM DENNIS FROM FATHER JACQUES MARQUETTE'S DESCRIPTION OF AN IMAGE ON A CLIFF OVERLOOKING THE MISSISSIPPI NEAR THE PRESENT-DAY TOWN OF ALTON, ILLINOIS THAT HE ENCOUNTERED IN AUGUST OF 1675.

and controlled storms, flood, and rain. On the northwest coast, the Haida and the Kwakiutl Indians feared the Sisiutl, sometimes depicted as a double-headed serpent and sometimes with four clawed feet, a snake-like tail, and a size large enough to swallow a full-grown man.

Further, strange as it may seem given their arctic range, the Inuit (Eskimos) also have their version of a dragon. The Inuit bands on Alaska's southern coast describe a huge reptilian sea monster looking something like a giant seagoing crocodile. Around Point Hope, the Inuit tell of the Kikituk, a large, saurian sea monster that comes ashore to eat humans and to hunt. In *Graphic Art of the Eskimo* (Hoffman 1897), we can see a number of images of dragonlike monsters etched on bone and ivory (figs. 11, 12).

In North Carolina and Tennessee, the Cherokee Indians and their neighbors tell of the *uktena,* an enormous horned water snake with a scaly body as big around as a tree trunk, horns on its head, rings or spots of color decorating its hide, a shining carbuncle mounted in its head, and wings (figs. 13,14). It was believed that to smell the *uktena's* breath would bring instant death.

Lawrence E. Sullivan, editor of *Native American Religions* (1989), wrote concerning the New World dragons, "Both in their form and in the role they played in the larger belief system, the 'uktena' and other serpentine monsters resemble both the feathered serpent of the Aztec and the dragon of Eurasia. Why these imaginary monsters should have been structurally similar remains to be explained" (142).

Dragons are universal, and the raptor/serpent/cat motif in the overall pattern of the dragon image and dragon tales, whether presented in Polynesia as *mo-o* or among the Cherokee Indians as *uktena* or among the peoples of India as *makara,* is easily recognized. The winged or flight-capable, scaled, and often clawed giant reptile with a mouth full of savage teeth is found everywhere, and so too are a number of recurring themes in the world-dragon tales: deadly breath, horns, crests, watery domains, danger to young women, jewel in the head, hideous roar, multiple heads, and staring or glowing eyes. But why? How can the universality of this strange complex of images and behavior be explained? What, if any, are the physical facts behind the universal dragon? And, finally, how can the behavior of African vervet monkeys help untangle the puzzle of the dragon?

Figure 11: AN ESKIMO DRAGON CONFRONTS A CARIBOU. NOTE THAT THE IMAGE OF THE GIANT LEGGED REPTILE OCCURS EVEN IN ARCTIC ENVIRONMENTS.

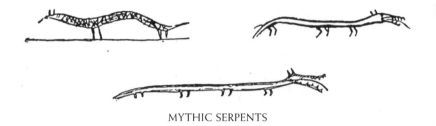

MYTHIC SERPENTS

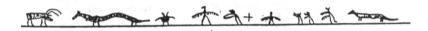

MYTHIC CREATURES

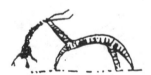

MYTHIC ANIMAL DEVOURING NATIVE

FIGURE 12: HOFFMAN, IN THE LATE 1800S, TOOK THESE ETCHINGS FROM VARIOUS INUIT BONE ARTIFACTS. NOTE THE MULTIPLE APPENDAGES ON SEVERAL OF WHAT HOFFMAN CALLS IMAGES OF 'MYTHIC ANIMALS' OR 'MYTHIC SERPENTS.'

Figure 13: DATING TO ABOUT A.D. 1200, THIS IMAGE OF AN AMERICAN INDIAN HYDRA DRAGON COMES FROM A CERAMIC VESSEL DISCOVERED AT THE SPIRO MOUND SITE IN EASTERN OKLAHOMA.

FIGURE 14: THE DRAGON OF THE SOUTHEAST INDIANS, THE *UKTENA* WAS ALWAYS FEATURED AS A LARGE, HORNED FLYING SERPENT. THIS IMAGE IS FROM A CERAMIC VESSEL FOUND AT THE MOUNDVILLE SITE IN ALABAMA.

THE MONKEY
HUNTERS

he world-dragon was formed by the nature of our own shad-
owy progenitors' encounters with the creatures who hunted
them over millions of years (fig. 15). To fully understand this
crucial period in evolutionary history, we must consider the primate
predators, the "primal" inspiration for the dragon, as well as the evolution
and nature of the primates. Although the basic outline of primate classification is generally accepted, numerous minor points vary from one
classificatory scheme to another. Since the minutiae of primate taxonomy
are not my interest, I will rely on the classification found in the most
recent edition of a commonly used textbook in the field of human evolution, William Haviland's *Human Evolution and Prehistory* (1994).

A standard disclaimer is required at this point. At issue is the reliability
of generalizing from ape and monkey behavior to human behavior or of
inferring ancestral primate behavior from that of the euprimates, or "primates of modern aspect." Anthropology generally assumes that studies of
the great apes, such as the chimpanzee and the gorilla—animals close to
us not only in genetic material but also, and not surprisingly, in behavior—
will shed insight into the social/cultural development of our most
ancient ancestors. However, nonhuman primates have evolved over time

FIGURE 15: OVER MILLENNIA, THE RAPTOR, BIG CAT, AND SERPENT BEGAN TO FORM AS A SINGLE CONSTRUCT—THE DRAGON—IN THE BRAIN/MIND OF OUR ANCIENT PRIMATE ANCESTORS.

just as humans have, and forms of behavior that modern primates exhibit may not have existed among their ancestors. Further, contemporary primatological studies have shown variations in primate behavior from species to species, and even within a particular group. These cautions must be considered when attempting to explain modern human behavior by evoking some putative ancient behavior, the existence of which is suggested by the fact that it is displayed by nonhuman primates. With these qualifying warnings in mind, we may proceed.

Primates belong to the kingdom Animalia, the phylum Chordata, the subphylum Vertebrata, and the class Mammalia. This means that they are classed with animals that experience live birth; ingest their food; are capable of voluntary motion; are warm-blooded; and possess sense organs, a backbone, hair, and mammary glands. The Platyrrhini, the New World monkeys, are native to Central and South America and are characterized by a flat nose, arboreal lifestyle, and prehensile tail. The Catarrhini consists of two superfamilies: Cercopithecoidea and Hominoidea. The Cercopithecoidea, the Old World monkeys, are recognized by their downward-pointing nostrils and their lack of prehensile tails. These animals may be tree dwelling or land dwelling and include baboons, Japanese macaques, rhesus monkeys, capuchins, and guereza monkeys. The Hominoidea superfamily includes the Pongidae and the Hominidae. The Pongidae are the Asian great apes. The Hominidae are chimpanzees, gorillas, and the subfamily Homininae: genus *Homo,* species *sapiens* . . . us.

The classification of humans, chimpanzees, and gorillas in the same family reflects the latest blood and protein chemistry studies, which establish that the three are more closely related to each than to the orangutan, for example. On the basis of tests with blood proteins, scientists have determined that the chimpanzee and gorilla are closest to humans, with the orangutan next, followed by the gibbons and siamangs, the Old World monkeys, the New World monkeys, tarsiers, and finally, at the greatest evolutionary distance from humans, the Strepsirhini. Humans and chimpanzees, for example, share at least 98 percent of their genetic material.

As far as can be known, primates are the only animals with a special historical rapport with the sources of the dragon image, and we humans, the most advanced primates of them all, have gone so far as to sustain the presence of the dragon through the entertainment industry, religion, arts, folklore, and mythology. This deep connection developed many millions of years ago, and to trace it we must look to the roots of our own kind, even considering the broader temporal context of those roots, for there is found the source and cause of the dragon.

Our planet came into being some 4 to 6 billion years ago. During the first half-billion or so years of Earth, we are told the planet was a tortured stone convulsed by volcanic forces, one great barren continent surrounded by a sea empty of life. About a billion years ago, microscopic life forms evolved that could sustain themselves by mixing oxygen and organic materials from plants and other forms like themselves. These were the first oxygen-breathing animals.

Over the next 400 million years, armored fish, the first animals to have a vertebral column, evolved, followed by small amphibians, who moved out of the sea to spend part of their lives on the land. Then, during the Carboniferous period, about 280 to 345 million years ago, reptiles and insects arose. In the succeeding Permian period, about 230 to 280 million years ago, fossils provide evidence that some reptiles were developing in a distinctive mammalian direction, and by the Triassic period, between 180 and 230 million years ago, true mammals were on the scene.

For the next several hundred million years, mammals remained small hunters of insects, grubs, worms, and eggs. Toward the end of the Cretaceous period, about 65 to 135 million years ago, the dinosaurs approached extinction, opening up many new ecological niches for the primitive mammals. As the ancient continents shifted, and warm, moist conditions over the planet favored the spread of huge forests, some of the insectivorean mammals experimented with an arboreal adaptation. Life in the trees naturally favored those animals that had the ability to judge distances through space accurately, and to grasp and hold on.

Then, during the Eocene epoch, some 34 to 55 million years ago, the temperature rose, causing the extinction of many older mammalian forms, which in turn were replaced by animals that modern humans could recognize.

During the Oligocene epoch, 23 to 34 million years ago, creatures resembling the tarsiers and the lemurs became somewhat dominated by the ancestors of the haplorhine primates; that is, they became more monkeylike, generally outcompeting more "primitive" primates. Then, some 22 million years ago during the Miocene epoch, the tree-dwelling, chimpanzee-sized ape called *Proconsul* evolved. Primatologists consider it ancestral to *Sivapithecus,* a Miocene ape that evolved 5 to 16 million years ago.

Of particular interest to those specialists who trace the twisting trails of human evolution are the environmental conditions that prevailed toward the end of the Miocene epoch. Rising temperatures and decreased rainfall resulted in a breakdown of the primal forests into a savanna-forest mixed environment. Two features then came into play. The populations of catlike predators grew in the savanna areas, making life difficult for the relatively small (forty to fifty pounds) sivapithecines. Further, experts hypothesize that some of the sivapithecines engaged in terrestrial hunting and gathering on the savanna, combined with strategic retreats into the nearby trees to eat, sleep, and find protection from predators. Obviously, those ancient primates who could gather food and then carry it to the trees had a survival advantage over their less talented comrades. Recent evidence suggests that apes and humans separated from a common ancestral line sometime during the late Miocene. Some of the sivapithecines evolved toward the human line, some in the direction of modern terrestrial apes, and some with a focus on life in the trees.

About 4.5 to 7.5 million years ago, the first hominine appeared. This fossil form, known as *Ardipithecus ramidus* and discovered in Ethiopia, is dated at 4.4 million years. Based on fossils from northern Kenya, known as *Australopithecus anamensis,* some anthropologists now suggest that *Ardipithecus ramidus* gave rise to *Australopithecus* somewhere between 3.9 to 4.2 million years ago.

The first member of the *Australopithecus* genus was identified in 1924 by Professor Raymond Dart of the University of Witwatersrand in Johannesburg. The fossil, found at the Buxton Limeworks near Taung, South Africa, was that of a three- to four-year-old juvenile, hence sometimes referred to as the Taung child (fig. 16). It drew Dart's attention because of the apparent mix of human and simian traits. Due to the position of the foramen magnum, the hole at the base of the skull through which the spinal cord passes, anatomist Dart argued that the creature was a biped—it walked on two feet—and named it Southern Ape of Africa, or *Australopithecus africanus.*

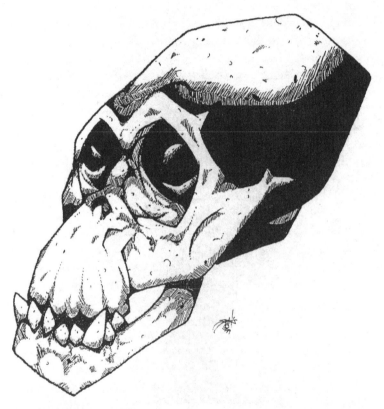

FIGURE 16: THE FOSSILIZED SKULL OF THE SO-CALLED "TAUNG CHILD," FOUND IN AFRICA IN 1924 BY ANATOMIST RAYMOND DART, WAS THE FIRST MEMBER OF GENUS *AUSTRALOPITHECUS,* THE ANCIENT LINEAGE OF HUMANITY, EVER IDENTIFIED. LATER STUDIES BY BERGER AND CLARKE IN 1995 DEMONSTRATED THAT THE ANCIENT CHILD WAS PROBABLY CAPTURED AND KILLED BY A RAPTOR SEVERAL MILLION YEARS AGO.

I have paused to consider the circumstances surrounding the find of the Taung child because a recent study by paleoanthropologists I. R. Berger and R. J. Clarke (1995), who like Dart worked out of the University of Witwatersrand, supports the notion that predators, in this case raptors, were significantly involved in behaviors that offer some answers to two of the continuing problems surrounding the Taung find. The first puzzle is that the Taung site has produced only the child's skull, whereas other similar sites—Sterkfontein, Kromdraai, Makapansgat, Swartkrans—have yielded several apemen fossils and associated artifacts. Secondly, the faunal assemblage—that is, the collection of animal bones found in association with the Taung child—manifests the presence of only small animals, many of which reveal unusual damage.

Competing theories suggest that the Taung faunal assemblage was caused either by a carnivore, possibly a leopard, or by water action. The argument that the Taung bone assemblage might have been washed into its present location by primordial stream patterns or flooding was dismissed on the following grounds: the geology of the site yielded no stream cobbles, nor did the bones show the wear of bones that had been moved any distance by hydraulic forces. A leopard as the collector of the bones was rejected because bone collectors, or bone chewers and gnawers like leopards, wild dogs, and porcupines, leave characteristic marks on their kills. None of these marks were found. Present on the Taung bone assemblage were the marks characteristic of the kills of large raptors such as the crowned eagle, the martial eagle, and the black eagle, identifiable V-shaped punctures left by the raptor's powerful beak. Finally, the Taung faunal assemblage is unique among all South African early hominid-bearing fossil sites because of the uniformly small animals represented and the relative scarcity of this type of animal remains at many other *Australopithecus* sites. Further, there was an absence of broken bones as one would find in the lair of a carnivore or early manlike creature. Berger and Clarke end their study by stating, "We thus conclude with the proposition that the Taung child and much of the associated fauna was killed and collected by a large bird of prey" (298).

With *Australopithecus* is found the first evidence of a large-brained, upright-walking primate with dexterous hands and fingers easily capable of rudimentary tool making. Its cranium was low, its brow ridges were large, and the lower half of its face was chinless. It probably spent some time in the trees, as do the modern great apes like the gorilla and chimpanzee, but it was clearly an advanced terrestrial primate. Then, about 2.4 to 1.5 million years ago, the first member of our genus, *Homo habilis,* appeared. The large-brained *H. habilis* was the first to create stone tools, known to archaeologists as Oldowan pebble choppers.

The preceding outline of primates and primate evolution offers the basis for the following discussion concerning primate predators and their evolutionary appearance. Since the major vervet monkey predators—raptor, leopard, snake—form the basis of my hypothesis concerning the roots of the dragon image among humans, the extension of this predator complex beyond the vervet monkeys must be explored and substantiated. If only the vervets were the targets of the raptor/leopard/snake predator triumvirate, the conclusion that the universal dragon is derived from a reaction to these primate hunters over millions of years would ring hollow. However, as we scan the globe and primate-predator relations, we see that the basic raptor/leopard/snake predator complex, with very few exceptions, is everywhere in the world where primates are found.

Among New World monkeys (Platyrrhini), the pygmy marmoset (genus *Cebuella*) of the upper Amazon, the smallest monkey in the world at about 4.4 ounces, is so at risk from raptors that it instinctively avoids the upper canopies of forests. This, however, puts it at additional danger from two of its other predators, snakes and cats. Likewise, Goeldi's monkey *(Callimico goeldii),* also found in South America, is hunted by birds of prey and big cats.

The capuchin monkeys of Central and South America, whose males average 7.25 pounds and females 5.7 pounds, are particularly susceptible to their predators, which include birds of prey, ocelots, and boa constrictors. Studies of jaguar predation in the Manu National Park in Peru indicate that a dietary focus of the big cats is black spider monkeys (Kitchener 1991, 137).

In Southeast Asia and the southwestern Pacific islands, clouded leopards, *Neofelis nebulosa,* specialize in the hunting of primates. In Sumatra they prey upon long-tailed macaques and will attack larger primates such as orangutans. In Borneo, proboscis monkeys and leaf monkeys contend not only with the clouded leopard but also with crocodiles, pythons, and black eagles.

The African great apes, although less susceptible to the classical triumvirate because of their larger size and group life, are still wary of the primate predators. In an area study at Mount Assirki in the Parc National du Niokolo Koba, Senegal, leopards pose the major threat to the chimpanzee population, with lions, wild dogs, and hyenas a close second. Leopards also prey on mountain gorilla populations. Due to the size of the great apes, raptors present no problem except to infants and juveniles, but poisonous snakes and constrictors present real dangers. Chimpanzees demonstrate innate predator-avoidance reactions to snakes and birds.

Old World monkey (Catarrhini) populations provide many examples of predation by the raptor/snake/cat complex. Blue monkeys *(C. mitis)* and red-tailed monkeys *(C. ascanius)* are hunted by leopards, eagles, and snakes, as are rhesus monkeys, patas monkeys, howler monkeys, white-nosed guenons, talapoin monkeys, and gray-cheeked mangabey monkeys. Leopards in the Amboseli area of east Africa are the major cause of death in the vervet monkey population.

Descendants of the ancient primate suborder Strepsirhini, which includes lemurs and lorises, are found in great number today only on Madagascar, the world's largest island, a land mass of 232,000 square miles lying off the east coast of Africa. The ancestors of today's lemurs were isolated on this island about 50 million years ago and have evolved in the absence of monkeys and apes.

Raptors are the major enemies of all types of lemurs. The mouse lemurs (genus *Microcebus*) of Madagascar are hunted by snakes, owls, and various types of cats and civets. Pottos, members of the loris family, are likewise prey of poisonous snakes, carnivores, and raptors. Tarsiers on Madagascar and elsewhere are typically hunted by hawks, eagles, mongooses, snakes, and cats.

Lemurs also demonstrate some exceptions to the pattern of predation reaction: they do not appear to be instinctively fearful of snakes. Alison Jolly (1966, 39) notes the absence of true poisonous snakes on Madagascar as a contributing factor to this atypical primate behavior. Likewise, red-faced Japanese macaques and baboons seem to have little predator anxiety. The large size of their social groups, the ecological niches they occupy, and—in the case of the baboon—their ferocious group response to threats may help explain this.

Another perspective on the relationship between primates and their predators can be gained by considering more closely the nature and history of the cats, raptors, and snakes that bedevil primates wherever they are found. Reptiles, the first full-time land-dwelling animals, appeared about 350 million years ago, and about 225 million years ago, toward the end of the Permian period, a group of now-extinct reptiles gave rise to the earliest mammals. One of the many ironies of evolution is that they would also become one of the mammals' major predators.

A brief survey of snakes that prey upon modern primates can offer insights into the age-old struggle between our most ancient ancestors and the snake. Some snakes are indeed daunting in size. The reticulated or regal python *(Python reticulatus)* from Malaya averages thirty-three to thirty-four feet in length, while the rock python *(Python sebae)* can reach over twenty-eight feet. The larger adults of this species can bring down small antelopes and are capable of killing and swallowing children and small adults. The largest known specimen of the tropical American snake the anaconda *(Eunectes murinus)* measured nineteen feet in length, thirty-six inches in circumference at the thickest part of its body, and 236 pounds in weight. Boa constrictors, of the family Boinae, which can attain twenty feet in length, are located all over the world and have been collected and studied in New Guinea, Australia, Asia, Malaysia, Africa, Mexico, India, and Madagascar.

A sample of monkey-killing snakes of Africa divulges the serpent horrors of the arboreal primate's world. The highly venomous Gabon adder *(Bitis gabonica)* from West Africa averages six feet in length, and adults will kill monkeys as well as hares, genets, and mongooses. Gold's tree cobra *(Pseudonhaje)* is a very poisonous serpent that reaches a length of seven feet and will attack arboreal mammals, including small, infant, and juvenile monkeys, as does Blanding's tree snake *(Boiga blandingii)* and the boomslang, *Dispholidus typus.*

Reptiles gave rise to primitive birds during the Mesozoic era about 180 million years ago. One of the first recognizable birds, the Archaeopteryx, evolved during the Jurassic period, some 160 million years ago. In the following Eocene period, the earliest known true birds of prey appeared. The oldest so far discovered, *Lithornis,* dates to 60 million years and was found near London, England. Birds of all kinds reached their peak about 500,000 years ago, at which time it is estimated (Everett 1976, 13) that the worldwide bird population was three times that of today.

Modern raptors, such as falcons, hawks, harriers, kites, vultures, and eagles, are grouped in the order Falconiform. The largest African raptor, the martial eagle, weighs up to fourteen pounds and possesses a wingspan of eight feet. Like the African tawny eagle, a somewhat smaller relative, it easily picks monkeys out of treetops and kills small antelopes on the ground.

The crowned eagle, smaller than the martial eagle but more powerful, feeds exclusively on mammals, including monkeys. In some parts of Africa, crowned eagles subsist entirely on monkeys—the vervet, samango, and colobus monkeys, with young baboons being the favored prey. Further, these eagles prey upon antelope such as bushbuck and grysbok, animals that weigh up to thirty kilograms. In 1982 in Zambia, a crowned eagle attacked and nearly killed a seven-year-old human child, and in Zimbabwe pieces of a juvenile human's skull were found in the nest of a crowned eagle (Berger and Clarke 1995, 280–81).

African black eagles, with wingspans over six feet, commonly hunt vervet monkeys and have been known to take small baboons as well as antelopes. One of their specialities is tortoise hunting. One pair of black eagles was reported to have killed eighty-four tortoises over a 119-day period by the interesting method of snatching the tortoise from the ground and then dropping it to its death from a height of thirty to sixty meters, after which the eagles dined. In the New World, the harpy eagle of Central and South America feeds on tree-dwelling mammals, including monkeys, as does the New Guinea harpy eagle and the huge Philippine monkey-eating eagle.

The first catlike carnivores, the so-called sabertoothed paleo-felids, appeared about 35 million years ago. By 20 million years ago, ancient species of big cats had spread to the Old and New World. Modern cats are in evidence from about 10 million years ago, in the late Miocene epoch, and the big cats of the modern genus *Panthera* appear about 2 million years ago in Europe and somewhat earlier in Africa.

Among the most ancient of the *Panthera,* leopardlike cats predate the appearance of lions by over a million years. The leopards lend importance to a discussion of primate predators because of their tree-climbing abilities; that is, their ability to threaten arboreal mammals. Leopards and jaguars had dispersed over Africa, Eurasia, Europe, and the New World by 1 to 2 million years ago. Other big cats—tigers, ocelots, lynxes, pumas, and cheetahs—were also radiating from their centers of origin at this time. The lion, as noted above, is a relative latecomer. Its oldest remains come from Bed II of Olduvai Gorge in East Africa and date between 500,000 and 700,000 years.

The leopard has adapted better than other big cats and can survive in virtually every type of habitat, from tropical rain forest to desert, from sea level to 5,000 meters above sea level. Its close relative, the jaguar, although confined to South and Central America today, resides in savanna regions, deserts, and tropical forests.

Leopards are very active, opportunistic, but not always successful hunters. Bailey (1993, 206) observed that the leopards in an African study successfully captured prey in only two of thirteen attempts. All daylight attacks failed, but the two night attacks succeeded. The diet of the leopards in Bailey's study, according to examination of their scats, was composed of about one-third small mammals, including monkeys. In a study of the scats of leopards in the Parc National de Tai in the Ivory Coast, monkey remains joined those of thirty different small mammals taken by the leopards (Kitchener 1991, 138).

Leopards often store their kills in trees, which brings them into confrontation with arboreal mammals. Bailey noted that of the fifty-five carcasses of animals killed by leopards in his study area, 84 percent had been placed in trees.

The preceding material suggests that the raptor/snake/cat primate-predator complex is universal and, further, that this deadly relationship began deep in the evolutionary history of our species. From Borneo to Peru, from Africa to India, from ancient times to modern day, primates confront their three basic predators on an almost daily basis and have been doing so all over the world for many millions of years. The success or failure of the primate to survive these encounters obviously has had a determining impact on the evolution of our kind of animal.

The effects of the primordial predator linger in the modern social and individual nature of contemporary primates. Today's primates stand larger than their ancient cousins because of their size advantage in daily battles to achieve sexual dominion, control over food, and choice resting areas within their own troop, as well as defense against the beasts that swooped down from the sky, leapt with claws unsheathed and teeth barred from ambush, or slithered quietly among the branches.

The social nature of primates and the pressure to evolve and maintain methods that make social cohesion more likely—the family, mutual grooming, food sharing, protopolitical structure, and so on—were also heavily influenced by the daily attacks of predators. The problem of the predator had to be resolved before any higher form of social development could occur. If life did not ensure relative safety and security, how could any form of behavior not directly related to self-defense evolve? Before art, before religion, before philosophy—before any of those distinctively "human" behaviors that our kind have developed over the millennia could become manifest—the issue of defense against the traditional primate predators had to be settled. Primates had to evolve significant alarm calls and innate and therefore automatic responses to alarm calls or to predator signature behavior—the writhing of snakes, the rush of the leopard attack, and the fluttering of bird wings—to assure that a sufficient number survived to maintain a steady rate of population.

Biologist Edward O. Wilson, in his extremely influential work *Sociobiology: The New Synthesis* (1975) wrote, "In higher primate species with multimale groups, organized defense is the rule. In fact, we can bring this generalization the other way around—the multimale unit may have evolved in order to provide coordinated hence superior defense" (46). And as primatologists Noel Boaz and Alan Almquist (1997) note: "Van Schaik (1983) believed that predation avoidance offered the only universal selective advantage of group living. They believe that predation is what sets the lower limit for group size." (231).

The dragon evolved from the same crucible that produced the most fundamental of human institutions, those that we share with almost all primates. In a way, the creature that we call "dragon" projects through cultural and individual artistic lenses as a primary feature of human evolution. Evolution is driven by natural selection, and natural selection does not work unless a threat exists in the environment to prevent an ill-adapted organism from passing along its genetic materials.

In comparing the evolutionary history of humans and that of three primate predators, one can discover when the roots of the dragon began to take hold. The first land-dwelling animals and the source of mammals, the reptiles, appear about 350 million years ago. The reptile/mammal relationship is, therefore, one of the most ancient predator/prey relationships in the animal world. The raptors evolved about 60 to 160 million years ago, at a time when the ancient rodentlike ancestors of the modern primates were experimenting with adaptation to life in the trees, and the big cats evolved simultaneously with the ancestors of the modern tarsiers and lemurs.

If *Sivapithecus,* which appeared about 5 to 16 million years ago, can be considered ancestral to modern primates, including humans, then we may note that the snake/cat/raptor complex was acting in relationship to ancestral primates, presumably as prey, for tens of millions of years before the appearance of our most ancient primate ancestor. The origin of the impulses that would lead to the world-dragon complex must have begun about 35 to 50 million years ago, when ancestral primates evolved in the dangerous company of raptors, snakes, and cats.

RUNNING FROM
CERTAIN SHADOWS

he dramatic responses of the vervet monkey to the three basic predator calls indicate not only the complexity of the monkey's psychobehavioral pattern, but also the critical significance of the instinctual life-saving behavior patterns that the predator calls elicit in vervet populations. The presence of the predator in primate evolution seems crucial in understanding how and why primate social groups formed and perhaps, by analysis of monkey call systems, how human language came to be. But if the universality of various behaviors is to be demonstrated, it must be shown not only that is it highly probable that primates have faced the same set of predators all over the earth from the most ancient times, but that the intensity of what was etched into their brain was also universally demonstrated in similar predator reactions. Is it only the vervet monkeys that display highly specific, and apparently innate, response to predator alarm calls, or is such behavior common in the primate world? If I am correct in the foundation of my hypothesis, it should be the case that some of the most complex patterns of behavior in primate groups (symbolic calls and stereotyped, complex physical responses) will be triggered by the presence of predators. Such responses (fear reactions, avoidance, withdrawal, freezing, movement into "safe"

FIGURE 17: THE RAPTOR, CAT, AND SERPENT, THE TRIAD OF PREDATORS
THAT HAVE THREATENED THE PRIMATES THROUGHOUT HISTORY,
CAME IN TIME TO FORM THE IMAGE OF THE DRAGON,
THE BEAST OF NIGHTMARES.

areas, running, climbing, hiding, and mobbing) should be fairly uniform across primate species, reflecting common experience and common results in the formation of the primitive awareness patterns of the primate brain—patterns that I feel formed the basis of the dragon image among humans (fig. 17).

One may ask, What good is fear? Why would an evolutionary selection process result in great fear in a particular species when a triggering event was encountered? In "What Good Is Feeling Bad? The Evolutionary Benefits of Psychic Pain" (1991), psychiatrist Randolph M. Nesse outlines his answer to this question by noting that of all the negative emotions, anxiety is the most obviously useful (228). Walter B. Cannon identified the fight-or-flight response, the best example of the value of anxiety, in 1915. From ancient times this response was of major benefit in the daily confrontation of prey and predator. When the predator attacks, the fight-or-flight response stimulates an accelerated heartbeat that more quickly pumps oxygen and nutrition in the form of blood glucose to the muscles, while at the same time speeding the removal of waste products. Muscle tension prepares the prey for an attempt to escape quickly or to stand and fight, while rapid breathing during the fight-or-flight reaction lends to the hyperoxygenation of the blood. Sweating concomitant with the fight-or-flight response serves to cool the body, and the secretion of adrenaline functions to energize the prey and to assist in the efficient clotting of blood should an injury occur. These physical changes also correlate with intense mental or psychological focus. In the midst of an attack by a powerful predator, the prey—at least the prey that has a chance to survive—will be strongly "in the moment."

Anthropologist Alison Jolly (1966), who studied several troops of lemurs in Madagascar, observed that whenever a hawk or other raptors were spotted, the lemurs roared an alarm call that triggered the troop members to look up, indicating that the particular call was specific to flying predators (39–40). Further, though gray parrots also shared the trees, the lemurs rarely issued alarm calls on a routine basis to them or any other birds, once more suggesting that their alarm call was voiced very specifically for the dangerous predators and only rarely for other birds (and sometimes airplanes).

Regarding another troop of lemurs in her Madagascar field study, Jolly noted that they issued their alarm only for hawks flying directly over the trees and rarely at high-flying hawks or airplanes (84). Further, the raptor calls sometimes prompted the lemurs not only to look up but to move quickly toward the ground and cover. Additionally, the lemurs' specific series of calls that warn of ground predators such as cats and baboons stimulated them immediately to climb high into the trees.

In 1993 primate researcher Joseph M. Macedonia and his staff studied the antipredator responses of forest-living lemurs over three years at the Duke University Primate Center in Durham, North Carolina. The constant proximity to the lemur troops allowed the research staff to provide a picture of lemur behavior under threat of attack from avian predators that illustrated the great complexity of their alarm calls and responses. Ringtailed lemurs, for example, issued warning calls when a large bird was seen at a distance. This "prewarning" call caused the other members of the troop to look toward the lemur who made the original call in order to ascertain the direction of the potential threat. If the bird was clearly identified as a raptor, the call and the response of the troop were different. If in the trees at the time of the close-proximity call, the ringtailed lemurs moved from the outside branches, where conceivably they could be attacked by a hunting hawk, toward the trunk of the tree. If the call intensified further, the troop moved down the trunk to the ground to seek cover. A different call signaled that a raptor was spotted in the vicinity but not focused on the troop as prey.

The responses of infant lemurs and their mothers to the above alarm calls were different again. In all cases, the various ranges of hawk calls stimulated the mother and infant to locate one another quickly. The infant would jump on the mother's back, and the mother would follow the general troop behavior, depending on the nuances of the raptor call and what it suggested (climb, look up, and so on). In several cases when the infants were in the lower branches of the undergrowth, the hawk calls stimulated them to release their grip and drop to the ground, where they would remain motionless as they made retrieval calls to their mothers.

Ruffled lemurs, when hearing the raptor alarm call, initiated a scanning behavior, quickly turning their bodies on the horizontal plane at 45-

and 90-degree arcs, alternating direction, as if preparing to meet an attacker but unsure of the direction from which it was approaching.

In one experiment a plywood silhouette of an attacking hawk was suspended over the lemur range. The lemurs in the immediate vicinity sent out the alarm call. Others in the area first looked toward the direction of the call, responded with their own calls, and approached the scene of the disturbance. They moved short distances—stopping, scanning, and moving again until they sighted the original alarm callers and the silhouette.

An adult female playing with an infant nearby responded to the silhouette by running to her infant, picking it up in her mouth, and climbing to a branch about twelve feet off the ground. She parked her baby there before returning to the ground, where she and the other adults emitted loud roars in the direction of the silhouette.

Ringtailed lemurs reacted to ground predators, dogs in the case of the Duke study, by immediately climbing the nearest tree. Young raccoons who wandered into the primate center from nearby woods, however, were mobbed; that is, the lemurs surrounded them and made threatening gestures as they roared and barked. In another experiment, a dog was slowly walked toward the lemurs and, in another, was presented in an ambushlike setting. In both cases the ringtailed lemurs indicated a ground predator with their alarm calls and were in the trees within seconds. Only the troop matriarch stood her ground against the dog. Though many times smaller than the dog, she bristled and growled at the approaching threat. The Duke lemurs treated snakes as minor disturbances, echoing the same type of alert but nonintense lemur response to snakes in the forests of Madagascar.

Like vervet monkeys and lemurs, capuchin, rhesus, and howler monkeys employ specific behavioral responses to predator alarm calls. Goeldi's monkeys with infants, for example, will at the sound of an alarm hide their babies in dense vegetation and flee, running and leaping in a random zigzag pattern to confuse a pursuing predator. Further, the escaping Goeldi's monkey will automatically move toward a lower layer of forest cover, too low to be captured by raptors and too high to be easily taken by ocelots and other hunting cats.

Fear, anxiety, and defensive reactions appearing in encounters with snakes are found among most primates species but are minimally present in some. In a famous experiment by psychologist Donald Hebb (cited in Konner 1982, 220), chimpanzee infants with no prior experience of snakes manifested extreme fear reactions when confronted with one. Another experiment with young and adult chimpanzees (cited in Marks 1987, 40) revealed that snakes, snakeskin, and crude snake models "terrified young and adult chimpanzees and evoked strong avoidance."

In another experiment (Morris and Morris 1965), snakes were introduced into the monkey house in a zoo. The monkeys shrieked and ran to the back of their cages, where they huddled together nervously, while the lemurs advanced to the front of their cages, curious about the snakes. Then again, some New World monkeys, like *Callimico goeldii,* may even hunt snakes on occasion. Snakes drive rhesus monkeys to display a sense of heightened alertness, avoidance, and even occasional aggressive defensive posturing and vocalizations, but seldom withdrawal.

Melville (1977) makes an interesting observation regarding movement and predators: "A fear of snakes is shown by most primates and is partly based on fear of their sudden, writhing movements. Human infants also show innate fear of intense, sudden or unexpected movement" (117). Primates fear more than the shape of their predator. Characteristic movements also suggest the predator's lethal identity—flapping and fluttering of birds, slithering of snakes, and the gaping mouth of the carnivore. Marks (1987), in discussing animal phobias in general, concurs that "sudden movements of the species evoke[s] particularly intense fear" (374).

Sluckin (1979) agrees: "A moving predator is often more likely to be responded to than a stationary one" (89). In the laboratory, two related experiments demonstrated the degree to which the primate's long relationship with its predators has left automatic survival-based responses in modern primates vis-à-vis strange or sudden movement. In the first experiment, young chimps proved reluctant to reach out of their cages for food if a nearby object moved whenever they tried, although they would reach for the treats if the object was not moving. A second experiment pointed out that the degree of avoidance, in this case the chimps shunning the food outside the cage, increased as the range of the moving object increased.

Such instinctual, or innate, responses to predators are not limited to primates. All species have them. A brief exploration of reactions to predators in groups other than primates will reveal different patterns in the response of prey to predators. At the same time, indirect evidence of the manner in which prey in general come to respond to certain aspects of the shape, movement, and general appearance of predators is offered.

The issue of innate fear response to movement requires the preceding brief survey because I believe that certain conventional features of the dragon—its horns, the multiheaded or "hydralike" dragon motif, and the "beards" found in some dragons—may result from identifying attack movements in the predator from the point of view of the prey.

RED TOOTH,
RED CLAW

he near-universal similarities in primate responses to the three basic predators of their order require an answer to the question, Why do primates respond to the "dragon complex" predators the way they do? The answer is to be found in evolutionary theory and natural selection. This theory best explains, at a physical and material level, how the dragon came to be.

The origins of the central tenets of evolutionary theory are well known. Charles Darwin worked with a long tradition of quasi-evolutionary thought that began hundreds of years before his time during the European Enlightenment—phrased then as the "idea of progress." These ideas carried forward into Darwin's time through the biological bent of Herbert Spencer's reading of "evolution," Edward Burnett Tylor's "cultural" evolutionary focus, and the geological discoveries determining the immense age of the earth championed by Charles Lyell and James Hutton.

Darwin, though he did not discover "evolution," did convincingly postulate how and why it worked. He argued for natural selection, the process by which environmental factors favor the survival of certain individuals and not others, thus ensuring that the genetic material of those individuals advances through the generations. Others, not favorably selected by environmental pressures, die out along with their heritable potential.

In 1865, just six years after the publication of Darwin's monumental *On the Origin of Species,* Austrian monk Gregor Mendel experimented with garden peas and discovered the working of genes and the answer to a question Darwin could not solve: How are variations passed from one generation to the next? In 1953 Francis Crick and James Watson demonstrated that genes are actually part of the DNA molecule (deoxyribonucleic acid) and that the arrangement of these molecular portions codes the information that determines the production of proteins, which in turn, for example, give the eyes one color and not another. Today, the combination of the most accepted and time-tested of the old and new ideas about evolution is called neo-Darwinian evolutionary theory, or "the modern synthesis." One aspect of this approach is biocultural anthropology (an umbrella term also covering sociobiology and evolutionary psychology), a series of research agendas that study the possible evolutionary or biological basis of universal human cultural behaviors.

Generally, anthropologists define *culture* as those conventional behaviors acquired through social learning. Biocultural anthropology is interested in understanding the potential biological basis of such "learned" behaviors. Otherwise stated, it investigates the nature of the interaction between some biologically etched pattern of behavior, usually construed as to have arisen through evolutionary pressures, and those behaviors that can be seen as relatively unique to a particular social group. To the question, Is it nature or nurture that channels how we evolve? the biocultural anthropologist answers with a resounding "Both."

The nature of family life (courtship, sexual patterns, domestic relations, child-rearing customs, management of resources, and so on) is widely conceived as primary in human evolution. Such a pattern assisted our tiny, helpless progenitors to survive by merging into family networks where everything from infant care to group defense to food could be shared. However, as biologically based as this fundamental pattern may be, as set in "nature," it is also true that cultural traditions exert great influences on the particular manner in which "nature" is expressed. Particular societies can present as normal a family form in which descent is traced through lines of women instead of men. The basic family pattern may be culturally transmitted to direct brothers to merge households, as among the Algonquin hunters of the Subarctic, or to suggest that a woman should have multiple ritual husbands, as among the Nyar of India, or that one can marry a chief's thumb, as is found among certain Northwest Coast Indian cultures. Sometimes the newly married couple is enjoined by custom to form a new household, while sometimes they naturally move in with the wife's family or the husband's or the mother's brother's.

As with the family, I think that the dragon impulse is primary. The forms the dragon takes—the artistic conventions that guide a particular culture to represent the biologically based beast in sculpture, painting, oral lore, and so on—are learned in a particular social grouping at a particular time. They will evolve on their own, not as a changing dragon but as changing artistic conventions. The inability to perceive the dragon as a biologically based creature with a great variety of styles of presentation has caused confusion among most dragonologists. The images of the dragon are not the dragon. Not acknowledging this is like attempting to box in the shadow of a tree as the sun runs its daily course, not understanding that the tree, not the shadow, is the crucial causal element in the shifting shapes on the lawn.

It is the search for the biological and evolutionary basis of the dragon that is of concern and not the use of the dragon as literary symbol or artistic motif. Obviously, if the world-dragon exists (in art, mythology, folklore) and is universal, it seems reasonable to hypothesize that the dragon is somehow related to the survival of those animals who possess it, or more properly, is related to its immediate causes in their repertoire of automatic recognitions of predators.

At its base, evolution works because of inheritable genetic variations in populations and individuals. The roots of observable traits arising in evolution are the genes, a word derived from the Greek word for birth. Genes are now understood as portions of DNA molecules, which are in turn located on long strands of DNA and protein called chromosomes that are found in the nucleus of each cell and are visible to the naked eye through light microscopes. Each chromosome contains the genetic material that determines the physical characteristics of an organism.

To understand evolution, one must move beyond the level of the individual, who does not physically evolve, to populations of individuals, a term in evolutionary parlance that refers to a breeding group. The total number of genes in the population is termed the gene pool. The physical, or phenotypic, future of a population depends upon the fate of the gene pool, a body that may be altered in a number of ways, such as by gene flow, genetic drift, and mutation.

Mutation, the ultimate source of genetic change, affects the gene pool by altering genetic materials at the cellular level. This change can occur spontaneously and randomly during the process of meiosis and mitosis or through environmental factors such as radiation, chemicals used in some fertilizers, food additives, and dyes. Mutation is important because it introduces variation into the gene pool, variation that could prove useful for a population's survival.

The various mechanisms by which gene pools are reduced or enhanced in complexity do not in themselves cause evolution, but rather they establish the materials with which evolutionary forces will work. A population's survival depends, of course, on its genetic makeup, but it is behaviorally delineated in terms of how well adapted to its environment that population may be. Adaptation can refer to a population's ability to access food resources, avoid predators, and successfully replicate itself over extended periods of time.

The key to evolutionary activity is the process of natural selection, the actual physical means by which a gene pool is affected by environmental pressures so that certain individuals rather than others are selected to produce the succeeding generation. Though many forces shape the nature of the gene pool of a population, natural selection hones and edits it through natural and, sometimes in the case of humans, cultural pressures. The population thus created is adapted to survive and reproduce successfully over generations because traits negative to its survival have resulted in the death of those carrying these traits and the elimination of a negative source of input into the future makeup of the genetic pool.

A classic example of natural selection at work is the case of the peppered moths of England. When first described by naturalists in the mid-1800s, the moths displayed a range of coloring from light to dark, with the lighter members in the majority. However, within several decades the dark-patterned peppered moths predominated, and the light-colored moths diminished rapidly. Over time the coloration of the English peppered moths shifted because of the growth of industrialization.

Prior to the building of pollution-belching industrial plants, the light-colored peppered moths blended with the light-colored lichens and bark on the trees they inhabited. Birds, their major predator, had a more difficult time seeing them against the light background of the trees but could see the darker moths, and therefore had a better opportunity to kill them. However, as soot and pollution darkened the trees, the light-colored moths, then increasingly visible, became easy targets for birds, while the darker moth population grew because its coloring was more adaptive. Presumably, as pollution is conquered and the discoloration of the moths' forest habitat diminishes, returning it to its naturally lighter bark coloring, the English peppered moth should once more show the dominance of the light-colored type.

Natural selection can quickly instigate changes in a gene pool, thus resulting in near-future changes in the shape and behavior of the population, which would tend to enhance the survival of the group. One researcher (cited in Barash 1977, 17–18) collected 136 sparrows that had been blown to the ground by a hurricane, and he took detailed measurements of the birds. Sixty-four died, demonstrating the effects of natural selection: the sparrows that survived had more compact bodies and shorter wingspans than the group killed in the storm. The birds with the longer wingspans, or more specifically the genes carried by those birds that resulted in a longer wingspan, were selected against by the conditions of the hurricane, while those birds with a tighter configuration lived to fly, and reproduce, another day.

The explanatory situation is somewhat different when we turn to a discussion of behavior that is seemingly hardwired in a species, as opposed to a situation—as with the peppered moth and hapless sparrows—where natural selection works for or against the continuation of genes that produce a certain phenotypical result (bodily characteristics). Both cases involve an increase in frequency of particular genes encoding for particular physical structure, not behavior, as a result of natural selection pressure. The key fact, however, is that in both instances the genes for the adaptive *and* the maladaptive traits were initially present together (i.e., both light and dark moths—and the genes encoding for these colors—were present before industrialization). Bio-behavioral evolution does not work in exactly that fashion, at least not among organisms that have complex nervous systems. Because these species inhabit complex and rapidly changing environments, their nervous systems must be able to respond flexibly and quickly. Initially, many—if not all—of these responses are *nongenetic*. However, if the behavioral "choice" works out, it is transmitted by animal learning and becomes a behavioral tradition. Under such circumstances, any mutation that would reinforce the behavior, for example, making it easier or more pleasurable to learn, would be selected for. This is called the Baldwin effect, or probable mutation effect. It is the mechanism of behavior-gene feedback that is in turn the central concept of sociobiology and biocultural anthropology.

A seemingly trivial behavior of the black-headed gull exemplifies another example of adaptive behavior. When their eggs hatch, black-headed gulls remove the pieces of shattered shell from the nest within minutes of the emergence of their chicks. At first glance, one could simply observe that most animals try not to foul their nests. However, if this behavior is viewed with an eye to its adaptive significance, another explanation presents itself—one that can be supported by experimentation.

The view guided by evolutionary theory suggests that the removal of the eggshells helps protect the chicks by making them less conspicuous to predators. The gull egg, though mottled on the outside and therefore somewhat camouflaged, is white on the inside. The white shells remaining in the nest draw predators, advertising the presence of helpless and tasty gull chicks. Of course, the gull parents who have the innate genetic propensity to clean their nests of newly broken shells serve to better ensure the immediate survival of their offspring, as well as pass along the complex of genetic heritage resulting from that cleaning behavior, which is derived from a more primordial pecking behavior.

An experiment in which gull eggs were set in nests and broken shells placed at varying distances from them supported the natural selection position. The closer the shell fragments were to the eggs, the more likely predators would find and attack the eggs (Barash 1977, 54–55).

Konrad Lorenz (cited in Marks 1987, 41), famed specialist in the study of animal behavior, performed an experiment in which he suspended a goose cutout from a revolving arm over a pen of newly hatched ducks and geese. When he flew the goose forward above the hatchlings, casting a "gooselike" (long-necked, short-tailed) shadow, they evidenced no escape responses. When he reversed the silhouette, the shadow of which then looked more like the typical short-necked bird of prey, the newly hatched brood, though they had never seen a flying goose or a hawk, instinctively reacted to the "hawk" with panic and harried attempts to find shelter. Again, the genetic materials that stimulate one goose to run immediately and another to respond more slowly to the silhouette of the hunting bird will ultimately result in the death of the slow to respond, and the greater productive potential of those goslings and ducklings hardwired through ages of natural selection to immediately flee the shadow of the hawk.

Experiments with snake-eating birds also demonstrate the manner in which natural selection polishes those behaviors that tend to augment the survivability of a species and delete those that do not. When sticks with alternating bands of color—imitating the deadly coral snake—were presented to hatchlings, they instantly panicked and attempted to escape, though they had never seen a coral snake. Unadorned sticks produced no effects. In a related experiment with motmots and great kiskadees, the birds were shown rods with colored stripes either running lengthwise or in bands of different colors. The birds avoided only the "coral snakes," the sticks with yellow and red bands (Smith 1975, 39).

Primate responses to predators and to dangerous situations can be argued to result from natural selection. Millions of years of nature shaping the worldwide primate population have resulted in a number of behaviors found in most primates that are directly related to the survival potential of groups and their members. In chapter 2, I discussed many primate behaviors that now can be understood as the result of natural selection. Madagascar lemurs instinctively look up and then move toward the ground and cover when an alarm call identifying the presence of a low-flying hawk is given. In the Duke University Primate Center studies, ringtailed lemurs, when hearing the raptor alarm call, moved from the outer branches of a tree toward the trunk; and if the call intensified, they, like their Madagascar relatives, moved to the ground and sought cover. Goeldi's monkeys, when alerted to potential predators, run and leap in zigzag fashion through the lower levels of the forest to confuse predator pursuit. They drop below the raptors' hunting range while at the same time remaining too high for the local hunting cats. Chimpanzee infants with no prior exposure to snakes react with fear and avoidance when confronted with a real snake, snakeskin, or a crude snake model. Baby rhesus monkeys and human infants instinctively withdraw when a projected shadow suddenly grows larger, and human infants become fearful when familiar toys are handled by researchers in such a way as to make the toy appear to rush toward them.

In each of the preceding cases, a behavior whose roots can, by the application of natural selection theory, be understood as a survival behavior shaped over thousands and thousands of generations is instinctively exhibited. Evolutionary mechanisms ensure that those primate individuals able to recognize the dangerous shape, the neighbor's alarm call, or strange, erratic, or rapidly approaching motion are more likely to survive and pass on their genetic materials than those animals who are not so responsive to the presence of predators or to the alarm calls of their troop. Those animals are killed, and thus eliminated as carriers of nonadaptive behavior.

Vervet monkeys, whose reactions to the three major primate predators first suggested the source of the dragon image, display a repertoire of behavior that through natural selection has developed their predator recognition competence and their ability to issue specific alarm calls with responsive behaviors specific to each. Those ancestral vervets who could not recognize the predator as quickly as their fellows stood at a disadvantage, as did those who too slowly grasped the significance and behavioral responses related to such calls. Those monkeys with successful predator recognition, predator calls, and predator escape behavior responses survived to pass on the potential of the adaptive responses through their genetic materials to the next generation.

HOW TIME
MAKES A DRAGON

he composite predator beast, the dragon, originates from three different animals—snake, raptor, cat—that have been in a predator/prey relationship with primates for millions of years. At a particular point in human evolution, a novel conception, "dragon," enters human consciousness. When is that point, and what is the means by which three separate pieces of behavior merge to become one fantastic panhuman image of a giant, many-toothed, winged serpent?

Several researchers in the field of communications theory—as well as those studying the problems of brain evolution, information processing, and memory—have proposed that the brain merges different but related items into single information-rich units as a natural process of its evolving. Apparently, it does this to keep up with increasingly complex input or changes in input due to the increasing complexity of environmental pressures on the organism, be that predator/prey behaviors or the necessity of learning and remembering larger and more complex bodies of cultural or technical information.

The observation that the mind merges or lumps like ideas into single units for more efficient processing goes back centuries. Famed philosopher John Locke, in his *Essay Concerning Human Understanding* (cited in Miller 1956b), states, "Wherein the mind does these three things: first, it chooses a certain number [of specific ideas]: secondly, it give them connection and makes them into one idea: thirdly, it ties them together by a name" (46).

George A. Miller of Harvard University, a specialist in communications, memory, and learning theory, explored a number of previously unconnected but related experiments in several scholarly papers he produced in 1956. Initially his research was triggered by his encounter with the "rule of six," a strange hardwired limitation in the brain that caused it to organize information around units of six. A variety of studies have shown that when humans scan the world around them, they can accurately perceive groupings of various types in terms of the number six or under, but beyond six, memory becomes confused and mistakes become more common.

In "Information and Memory" (1956b) Miller wrote of his first encounter with a digital computing machine and the men who operated it. Twenty small lights on the display panel would indicate the relays operating at a specific time. Miller was interested in the manner in which the machine operators could remember the many variations of illuminated and unilluminated lights on the twenty-light panel. He found that rather than relying on memory for the patterns and their great number of permutations, the workers grouped the lights into units of three and assigned a single number as its "name." When three contiguous lights were off, the identifying number was not (000) but rather 1. When a tripartite unit showed an off-off-on pattern, or (001), it was dubbed 2; and when the pattern was off-on-off, or (010), it was called 3; and so forth. Using this method, the computer workers could, for example, break down a string of fifteen on and off patterns into only five sets of three. As Miller noted, "Reorganization enabled the engineers to reduce the original complexity to something easily apprehended and remembered without changing or discarding any of the original data" (43).

In another experiment cited by Miller (1956a), subjects could remember on the average five words from a longer list. Each word was composed of three phonemes, linguistic sounds that make a difference to the listener in terms of discriminating one word from another. The words *jones, bones,* and *zones* indicate that *j, b,* and *z* are phonemes because when added to -*ones,* three distinct words are recognized by the English speaker. The research subjects obviously reacted as if they were responding to five words, not fifteen phonemes. They could remember five words from a list but not fifteen consecutive phonemes, even though the information conveyed was identical. Miller comments, "We are dealing here with a process of organizing or grouping the input into familiar units, or chunks, and a great deal of learning has gone into the formation of these familiar units" (93).

Chunks are, in Miller's parlance, not merely a group of items but a group that has psychological significance, that is, a grouping that will elicit a recognition and response. In the preceding example, the phonemes— *j, b, z*—have no meaning in themselves, but as *jones, bones, or zones* (a chunk of information, words in this case), their meaning is both recognized and conveyed. John E. Pfeiffer (1982) comments,

> The result is the formation of hierarchies of remembered units, complexes of lumped-together information. This process, known as "chunking," is the secret of our voluminous memory capacity. It is a way of beating the apparent limitations of the rule of six by successively more compact packaging, by cramming more and more information into a small number of readily recognized units, and then building other units into still more compact systems, patterns of patterns. (215)

Pfeiffer brings the discussion into a decidedly anthropological dimension when he writes,

> If their art is any indication, the people of the Upper Paleolithic were acting precisely in accordance with this principle. Confronted with an increasingly complex way of life and a pile-up of information, they were engaged in the first large-scale effort to organize knowledge for readier long-term retention and recall. The effort called for the invention of symbols, entire repertoires or vocabularies of symbols, in a burst of chunking. (215)

Borrowing language from communication theory, Miller also writes about the process of recoding. He notes that when beginning telegraph operators are attempting to learn Morse code, they initially focus on *dit* and *dah* as separate chunks. In time, they group these two chunks into one chunk, the letter. *Dit-dah* is *A. Dah-dit-dit* is *B. Dah-dit-dah-dit* is *C,* and so on. Then the letters are organized into words. As the chunks become larger, the messages that the telegraph operator can remember increase. In communication theory, this is referred to as "recoding." The operator receives a message of *dits* and *dahs,* a message with many chunks but with little content, or bits, per chunk. The operator reorganizes, or recodes, the input into another code with fewer chunks but more bits per chunk. What is happening here is that input events are grouped, and a new name is applied to the group, thereby lessening the amount of information that needs to be processed without limiting the quantity of bit content.

In "How Big Is a Chunk?" (1974) Herbert A. Simon explores the mechanisms of memory and proposes the means of identifying the basic human memory units, a process he arrives at by combining information from several experiments. In discussing EPAM, or elementary perceiver and memorizer learning theory, he comments on this theory's orientation to the problem of understanding human memory processes: "In the EPAM theory, fixation is identified with assembling compound symbol structures from components—a familiar notion from association theory—and storing the compound structures in memory, appropriately 'indexed.' ('Indexing' simply means storing information that permits recovery of the compound structure upon recognition of its stimulus components)" (485).

EPAM theory holds up the notions of "fixation" and "indexing" to suggest something structurally analogous to Miller's "chunk." Both cases suggest that the brain stores complex memory packages—"compound symbol structures [derived from] components," as Simon puts it.

The conception of some kind of patterning, or significant grouping, in brain activity is also advocated by brain researcher Donald R. Griffin in his *Animal Thinking* (1984), when he posits that consciousness is caused by patterns of activity involving thousands of neurons. David J. Chalmers (cited in Franklin 1995, 30ff.) also spoke of consciousness as "patterns" of neural activity.

Griffin suggests the term *template* for a particular "sensory pattern" (Franklin 1995, 53) and further notes that these sensory patterns can be biologically inherited. To explain his position, he offers this brief discussion of the behavior of the caddis fly. In that genus, the larvae will construct protective cases from grains of sand, cut vegetable materials, and mud, as well as their own sticky silk. Each species of caddis fly constructs its own particular species-specific type of larvae cases. The interesting point is that if a part of the larvae case is broken off in nature or is removed by an experimenter, the larvae will find the appropriate materials and cut them to fit the missing piece. Some type of inherited template—species-specific caddis larvae cases—must exist in some fashion in order to guide the larvae in its scrupulous maintenance of a particular type and shape of case, as opposed to repairs that would perhaps solve the damage to the larvae cases but not in a preordained or species-specific fashion.

With regard to examples of human templates, Griffin writes (in Franklin 1995), "We apparently have built-in language capabilities. What form do these take? I suspect that some of it might be in the form of templates, but of course not visual templates. Such templates might, for example, somehow bias us toward the use of syntax, or toward attaching names to our categories" (53).

Earl Count (cited in Laughlin, McManus, and d'Aquili 1992,70) coined the term "biogram" and used it to identify "the bundle of adaptations, social relations, and behaviors that are transmitted genetically and are thus characteristic of particular species and phyla. . . . The human biogram may be seen as an evolutionary transformation of the primate biogram, which is in turn a transformation upon the mammalian biogram, and so on down the phylogenetic scale."

Franklin (1995) speaks of "neurognostic structuring," a pattern of brain activity that, for example, results in the "predisposition to nurture infants" by "triggering the neurocognitive structures mediating recognition and response to 'babies' " (70). Simon (1974) refers to Miller's use of the "chunk" concept as "artfully vague" and cites Miller to demonstrate his point (482). "The contrast of the terms *bit* and *chunk*," writes Miller, "also serves to highlight the fact that we are not very definite about what constitutes a chunk of information." But, as I have noted earlier, Miller's "chunk" and "recoding," Simon's observations concerning elementary perceiver and memorizer learning theory's use of "fixation" and "indexing," Griffin's use of "template," Chalmers's "patterns of neural activity," Count's "biogram," and Franklin's "neurognostic structure" point to the same general principle. Whether the research is based on experiments in memory or hypotheses concerning the functioning of the nervous system, consciousness and brain function assume the fundamental principle that the brain groups, collapses, organizes, patterns, or structures complexes of general behaviors and information.

Miller (1956a) suggests that such groupings of information had survival value for our primal ancestors:

> We might argue that in the course of evolution those organisms were most successful that were responsive to the widest range of stimulus energies in their environment. In order to survive in a constantly fluctuating world, it was better to have a little information about a lot of things than to have a lot of information about a small segment of the environment. If a compromise was necessary, the one we seem to have made is clearly the more adaptive. (88)

Perhaps the dragon can be viewed as "a little information about a lot of things." Then the specific predator calls and responses of animals like the vervet monkeys would be comparable to "a lot of information about a small segment of the environment."

The dragon is an expression of such chunks, indexings, biograms, and neurognostic structure—a brain-dragon that was created during the time when our ancient arboreal ancestors were adapting to a life on the ground. The deeply etched patterns of recognition and responses to the three major predators, honed among arboreal primates for millennia, were lumped at this point into a general predator category, the culturally phrased expression of which is "dragon." The raptor, reptile, and tree-climbing carnivore alarm and response patterns are three basic patterns of behavior comprised of numerous smaller ones. The evolution of "dragon" is like the "operator" recoding input into few chunks with more bits per chunk; i.e., the dragon is a much more complex image than is snake, or cat, or raptor. Miller (1956) writes, "There are many ways to do this recoding, but probably the simplest is to group the input events, apply a new name to the group, and then remember the new name rather than the original input events" (93). It might be said that the "new name," or brain-file label, is "dragon." The "original input events" are the hard-wired behaviors related to each of the three predators.

It can be assumed that the dragon's embryonic existence began toward the end of the Miocene epoch, some 5 to 23 million years ago, when rising temperatures and decreased rainfall transformed the primal forest into a mixed environment of open plains, or savanna, and forest. The "dragon" was probably fully fixed 3 to 4 million years ago, about the time of *Australopithecus,* the first large-brained, upright-walking primate with the manual dexterity to make stone tools.

The dragon complex in the evolving primate brain developed slowly as climatic and environmental changes led to conditions where previously arboreal animals had to move from the trees and cross open areas to find food. This led them to face more predators who would have a better chance of successfully attacking and eating them. Natural selection favored the larger animals: a martial eagle cannot, for example, pick up an adult chimpanzee, an animal roughly comparable in size to the earliest of the upright walking prehumans. Snakes became somewhat less of a problem as the evolving upright posture and longer legs for running enabled the ancestral primate to assume elevated postures to more clearly see the snake before it could strike. The terrestrial carnivores like the big cats came to have more to fear from a traveling band of primates and would only prey upon the unattended juvenile or rarely solitary adult. Today, for example, an African leopard will almost always turn away from an approaching band of chimpanzees.

The complete brain-dragon complex appears at this point in primate/human evolution because of the same theoretical assumptions that seek to explain why the more ancient specific predator responses would have arisen in the first place—natural selection. It would be clearly adaptive for a monkey population to evolve specific predator call and responses, whereas such a generalized predator referent as a "dragon" call for arboreal animals would be, in fact, maladaptive. The raptor call elicits an immediate life-saving response, whereas a general predator call—dragon in this case—would simply freeze the hearer with a signal that means "very, very dangerous" or "be very afraid." This call would give no specific escape information, as does a raptor call or the sight of a nearby large hunting bird, but the resulting freezing would, in most cases, give the advantage to the attacker. The line between life and death can be measured in fractions of a second: the swoop of a hunting eagle, the strike of a cobra, the sudden lunge of the ambushing leopard. Any behavior that prolongs immediate reaction time to a predator would be dangerous to the population. "Dragon," therefore, had to be born after the initial stimuli, which led to the shape of the dragon in cultural expression, were no longer of immediate survival reality to the now terrestrial ape-like ancestors of modern humans.

This creation of the merged composite predator image, the dragon, may differ from the patterning assumptions characteristic of the ideas of Miller, Count, Chalmers, and company. The pattern of which I speak could result from a merger based on the decay or nonfunction of earlier behavioral patterns, which in their isolated form were definitely adaptive or functional. The idea that the dragon is some type of decaying structure is suggested by its generalized nature, the low level of human anxiety that now greets the dragon image, and its plasticity of cultural renderings, or perhaps it was due to inhibitory inputs from an enlarged cortex. More specific brain triggers are, like the predator calls of the vervets, not generalizable and very specific to a certain stimulus. It seems that as prehumans evolved and arboreal predator fears became less stringent, the three-predator alarm/response system broke down by first abandoning the features common to all three—fear, preparation to act immediately, and anxiety—and lumping them into an index about maximum fear, anxiety, and immediate response requirements. At the same time, the salient features of each of the three predators were retained and then merged, which in a manner of speaking is more "space-" and energy-efficient in the brain.

A discussion of animal phobias in modern human populations will grant some insight into the deep biological basis of the dragon. It would seem likely that the cause of the dragon, if it is as biological and ancient as it seems, would be seen in the behavior of modern-day humans. This turns out to be the case.

A phobia expresses an excessive fear reaction that might be understood in terms of three components: subjective, autonomic, and motor. Subjectively, when confronted with the fear-evoking stimulus, a phobic individual will experience intense and immobilizing fear. Some victims report they feel like they are dying, while some feel as if they are suffo-cating, and still others describe the sensation that they are about to faint or collapse.

Autonomic responses include rapid respiration, sweating, trembling, palpitations, muscular tension and/or weakness, involuntary excretion, breathlessness, nausea, and dry mouth. The behavioral, or motor, response to intense fear will be flight from the stimulus or the inability to move, "frozen" by fear. Specifically, the biocultural argument for the dragon is supported if the raptor-snake-carnivore complex makes an appearance in the phobias of humans.

Before the age of six months, human infants show very little fear. After this, animal phobias can manifest in children with no apparent trau-matic origin. Even though snakes are very rare in the British Isles, for example, one-third of British six-year-olds have been found to be afraid of them (Rachman 1968, 19ff.). Most animal phobias begin in early childhood. Between two and six years of age, children most commonly fear snakes, birds, and cats—the dragon complex.

Psychiatrists M. G. Gelder and I. M. Marks (1966, 309–19), in a study of phobias in a sample of 139 patients, noted that a fear of birds and cats was typical and that most of the subjects experienced this fear before they reached the age of five. Psychologists P. J. Lang and A. Lazowik (cited in Rachman 1968, 37) studied a population of students in Pittsburgh who were treated for intense snake phobia. Contact with snakes in this area is highly unlikely; however, all the subjects admitted to an intense fear, a claim substantiated by Lang and Lazowik by exposing the students to snakes in the laboratory.

Another study (Agras, Sylvester, and Oliveau 1969, 151–56) found that in a population of 1,000 subjects, 390 will exhibit fear of snakes, the highest incidence in a listing including heights, storms, death, injury, and enclosures. An average of 307 per 1,000 feared heights. Isacc M. Marks (1987, 15) writes that in most countries the human dread of snakes is dis-proportionate to their danger, and when speaking of "natural" phobias, the first on his list is the snake. He includes birds and feathers as prime examples of animal and animal-related phobic triggers and notes that the most common in the clinic is the fear of birds and spiders. In a discus-sion of monosymptomatic phobias of animals, Matig Mavissakalian

(1981) notes as examples "fears and avoidances of dogs or *cats, birds or snakes* [emphasis added], as well as particular situations such as thunderstorms, darkness, and heights" (5–6).

The modern psychological residue of the ancient predator/prey relationship between primates and the dragon-complex predators is profound, still present, and multifaceted. Humans have many innate responses that can be understood as based in evolutionary responses to natural selection vis-à-vis predators. In a series of experiments (Haslerud 1938) human toddlers became immediately fearful of familiar toy animals if the toy "rushed" at them, that is, was moved by a researcher toward them in a looming manner. When at rest, the toys were handled by the children with no apparent anxiety. In another experiment (Russell 1979) rhesus monkeys and human infants grew wary and tried to move away when a shadow projected on a screen before them was quickly enlarged, generating the illusion of a looming attack from close proximity.

Marks (1987) writes, "Animals, be they tubeworms or men, withdraw from sudden touch" (34). N. Tinbergen (1969) says with regard to the reaction to touch, "The touch stimuli given by an insect crawling on the skin release the response of throwing it off with a quick movement of the hand. This movement contains both a fixed pattern and an orientation component, and is, therefore a reaction of greater complexity than a mere reflex. It is probably innate and matures relatively late. It is accompanied by a subjective phenomenon, disgust" (209).

If touch is not avoided in the predator attack, capture of the prey follows. But here again, the innate response of the prey is to struggle, an act that if vigorous enough and timed correctly could produce freedom from capture. If the prey does not struggle, however, it is surely doomed; thus nature selects for animals that withdraw when touched and struggle when seized.

Marks (1987) notes that "fear of two staring eyes is widespread throughout the animal kingdom. The more conspicuously eyelike the markings, the more they deter" (35). A. D. Blest (1957) performed an experiment in which small birds were encouraged to approach a feeding tray baited with dead mealworms. As soon as the birds alighted, a circuit was completed that lit a design pattern of crosses, parallel lines, or circles immediately beneath the mealworms. The researchers found that the birds flew away more readily from the circular patterns than from the crosses and parallel lines, and that the more the circles were made to look like eyes, the more potent they were in stimulating rapid escape in the birds.

A number of researchers point out that sudden, strange, or loud noises also trigger fear in human infants. A. T. Jersild and F. B. Holmes (1935) report that young children, unlike adults, tend on the whole to fear tangible objects (e.g., real animals and noises). Marks writes (1987), "Fear is triggered by many stimuli generated by predators and conspecifics. Among these stimuli are abrupt movement nearby accompanied by sudden noise (like the pounding of feet or beating of wings), as well as stimuli more characteristic of only a few species" (34).

One of the most common phobias, agoraphobia, a word derived from a Greek phrase that literally reads "fear of the marketplace," may be related to evolutionary stresses and predator responses. Agoraphobics exhibit a fear of going into open public places. Walking alone or being alone compounds the fear categories of the agoraphobic. Those who have studied this very common phobia have come to think that agoraphobia may be more about a fear of one's own inefficient responses to certain situations than a specific reaction to open places. A. J. Goldstein and D. L. Chambless (1978) have even suggested that the central fear in agoraphobia is the "fear of fear."

Many studies have demonstrated that when rodents find themselves in an open space, they react with anxiety and immediately seek cover. If none is available, they will seek a "wall" and press themselves against it, a behavior called "wall clinging" in rat behavior studies. A related experiment found that rats in an enclosed open area will always move to the periphery of the open space. W. Sluckin (1979) observes, "Prey species in which antipredator behavior depends on cover in the form of vegetation, burrows, etc. may be expected to avoid open, exposed places, since these increase the chance of being spotted and decrease the chances of successful evasion" (110).

The survival value of agoraphobic behavior can be easily understood as a result of natural selection for behaviors that would lead an animal to avoid the dangers of open spaces, a zone where the ancient primates were helpless before the attacks of raptors, snakes, and cats. The fear of being alone and the "fear of fear" is also understandable in the context of predator/prey relations. The lone primate presents a relatively easy target for a number of predators, but when in groups, the prey can withstand the stalking predator. Likewise, the "fear of fear," or the fear of the ineffectiveness of one's own reactions in a given situation, is understandable in that such a situation would cause the animal to panic, impeding its ability to react with smooth haste to escape danger.

The comments of therapists concerning treatment of the agoraphobic tend to support the suggested predator/prey origin of the syndrome. Many agorophobics are helped by using a stick, pram, shopping cart, or dog. Further, anxiety decreases in the dark or under an overcast sky or when wearing dark glasses and sucking strongly flavored sweets.

The "stick" as a means to dispel fear is instinctual and is commonly seen among chimpanzees in their defensive maneuvers against attacks by carnivores. The pram, shopping bag on wheels, or dog is the artificial creation of the safety of a group, a "more than one alone" situation. And in the darkness, or even in the suggestion of darkness produced by dark glasses or an overcast day, the ancient prey within feels some relief from the potential surveillance of the hunting predator. Darkness or dimness signals relaxation and safety, while bright lights can suggest danger. Witness the classic use of the bright, unremitting light in stereotypical scenes of police interrogation or the use of lights that are never turned off in brainwashing techniques. Connect a bright, glaring, constant light and isolation of the primate from its comrades, and the ingredients to mentally "break" any primate—monkey, ape, or human—are in place.

Another series of classic experiments, though not directly related to animal phobias, shows how natural selection has worked to create an innate fear of heights in primates and other animals. The survival value of avoiding open space, which from the perspective of primate arboreal origins is a more likely interpretation of the "fear of heights" experiment, is obvious. The more arboreal animals can detect empty space beneath themselves and avoid it, the more likely they are to survive and pass on their genetic inheritance. This presumably includes sensitivity to finding oneself with no surface underfoot, a condition that would produce death or injury to our arboreal ancestors.

The format of the "visual cliff" experiment is set up as follows. A sheet of transparent plastic or glass is elevated a foot off the floor, with a patterned material attached to the underside of half the sheet. Patterned material is also placed on the floor beneath the glass, leaving the visual impression of a shallow side and a deep side to animals placed on the transparent surface. A variety of experiments have been performed with the "visual cliff." Many land-dwelling species—chicks, rats, goats, lambs, pigs, dogs, cats, monkeys, and human infants—when placed on the boundary between the deep and the shallow sides, move onto the shallow side and away from the deep side. When placed on the deep side, kittens and young goats become tense and freeze, while baby monkeys exhibit a number of fear reactions such as crouching, calling, and self-clasping. On the other hand, aquatic species such as ducks and turtles typically venture onto the deep side.

Conclusions from research concerning such factors as the age at onset of animal phobias, the age of predictable remission, and observations about the gender of animal phobics are well documented. Most animal phobias originate in childhood. Before puberty, animal phobias are found in both boys and girls, but they dramatically decrease by the age of ten or eleven, and this decrease is more apparent with boys than girls. Rachman (1968, 18) notes that fears of animals, though very common in childhood, show a high spontaneous remission rate. Further, animal phobias are generally easily treated by simple exposure therapy. Interestingly, animal phobias are seldom associated with other psychiatric disorders.

The origin of animal phobias generally puzzles therapists, as does the fact that though most patients overcome their animal phobias in the course of their maturation, some do not. Rachman (1968, 31) believes that "phobias are learned responses"; however, Dr. Isaac M. Marks (1987, 374) disagrees. He notes that the majority of animal phobias begin in childhood with no convincing traumatic origin and that only 23 percent of a related sample identified the onset of the phobia with some terrifying encounter with an animal. Further, he writes that in that 23 percent, no child experienced pain in the animal encounter. He concludes that young children seem prepared to develop intense fears of animals with little or no cause.

Sigmund Freud, likewise, was unsure of what childhood animal phobias indicated. He wrote (cited in Marks 1987),

> The child suddenly begins to fear a certain animal species and to protect itself against seeing or touching any individual of this species.... Sometimes animals which are known to the child only from picture books and fairy stories become objects of the senseless and inordinate anxiety which is manifest in these phobias. It is seldom possible to learn the manner in which such an unusual choice of anxiety has been brought about. (374)

Sometimes an event that triggered an animal phobia will be discovered in therapy, but the particulars of the event appear problematic to the therapist. In one reported case (Marks 1987), a feather phobia began when an infant was startled by a strange woman with a large feather in her hat bending over the carriage to look at him. The researcher commented, "Why the ensuing phobia was of feathers, rather than of the prepotent stimulus of strangers, remains a mystery" (374).

Most animal phobias can begin without the traumatic triggering event typically searched for in therapy. Young children simply appear preconditioned to acquire intense fear of animals with little or no cause. Freud noted that animals never directly experienced, but perhaps learned of through fairy tales, can be the base of the anxiety and fear of the animal phobia. He concluded that it is seldom possible to learn the manner in which such an unusual choice of anxiety has been brought about. Marks surmises that the fear of animals unmet must come from some behavior other than direct conditioning and weakly concludes that the fears are presumably passed on verbally by parents. In the case of the stranger with the feathered hat startling an infant and creating a fear not of strangers but of feathers, the choice mystified the therapist.

All of the above quandaries can be resolved if it is allowed that humans, through the long experience of their arboreal primate forebears have—through natural selection for behaviors that limit the success of the classic primate predators and increase the adaptive fit of the population—derived automatic behaviors that rendered avoidance and anxiety related to primal predators a deeply etched feature of the human brain. No traumatic event in the life of the child need exist for the ancient predator responses to find expression. Freud's conclusion that the precise cause of the animal phobia is seldom possible to learn is flawed because he was looking in the wrong place for the cause. It is found rooted not in the contemporary psychological life of the victim, Freud's hunting ground, but in the evolutionary history of the species. Why the feathers and not the stranger became the fear fixation of the child in the baby carriage may be related to the primates' age-old relations with the raptors, apparently a more profound and deeply based fear than that of strange humans. Raptors and arboreal primates engaged in a death struggle many millennia before the evolution of the human and the possibility of the human stranger.

Three features of animal-phobic behavior throw additional light on the suggested decaying, or perhaps only highly generalized, nature of the brain-dragon. First, not everyone is an animal phobic; in fact, most are not. Second, an individual can be afraid of snakes but not of birds or large animals; and third, it is relatively easy to cure an animal phobia. Whereas fear reactions to height in the "visual cliff" experiment and reactions to reflex stimulation (knee-jerk reflex, foot- and hand-clenching reflex behavior in newborns, closing the eyes when one sneezes, and so forth) are uniform across the board, animal phobias are not. It is as if the iron grip that innate predator calls have on the uniform reactions of arboreal primates has weakened through time. The pattern does remain in the cultural expressions of the dragon and in the continuing confusion of psychotherapists in understanding the cause of animal phobias when typical psychoanalytic causes such as traumatic conditioning do not fit the case.

Likewise, the vervet monkey case and others show that all the population respond equally to all the predators, but in humans the animal phobia is selective. One patient fears feathers, is only mildly anxious around snakes, and in fact loves cats and dogs. Another fears furry animals but loves snakes. Generally, modern psychotherapeutic literature yields little evidence of an individual showing intense fear of birds, snakes, and carnivores.

Lastly, a further example of the weakening of the basic complex is found in the fact that the animal phobia is one of the easiest to cure. On the other hand, fear of heights and agoraphobia may be extremely difficult to impact in the therapeutic setting, and reflex behaviors are almost definitively impossible to "cure," or stop.

Animal phobias in humans suggest that the brain-dragon can exist while specific animal phobias may continue to function. Here may be evidence that orders of magnitude of stimulus/response exist. The same brain structure may contain information that causes fear of serpents and at the same time have a generalized label, or a high-level categorization or index, as "dragon." In the earlier example of the instinctual behavior of the caddis fly, it was seen that the fly has a general pattern that might be labeled "larval case," which allows it to instinctively create such cases, an indispensable feature of its life cycle and existence. In addition, the caddis fly can also respond to repair on parts of the cases, even possessing the specific information to re-create pieces that could have countless variation in size and shape. Obviously, this underscores the fact that the brain could not store specific responses to every possible permutation of "missing fragment" of a caddis-fly larval case. Thus both the general and the specific information maintain existence in the caddis-fly brain. It can respond to the big picture and to pieces of the picture.

Similar is the beaver's amazing instinctive ability to build hydrodynamically correct dams and lodges. The beaver might be said to have a pattern called "lodge and dam in moving stream." The beaver clearly can deal with minute pieces of the larger picture—reacting to specific water conditions such as depth, temperature, and rate of flow, as well as to forest cover amenable to beaver dam or lodge construction—through genetic programming available to all successful members of the species.

W. Sluckin (1979) makes an interesting point: Phobias of such things as knives, hammers and electrical appliances are very rare or nonexistent, despite the fact that they are quite likely to be associated with pain or other trauma. This leads to the suggestion that certain stimuli and stimulus features are more readily associated with fear-evoking stimuli than are others as a result of preparedness through human evolution (124).

The dragon evolved as a presence in the brain about 3 to 4 million years ago, when our ancient ancestors abandoned arboreal life and adapted to life on the ground. This process, the creation of the brain-dragon, took place over many hundreds of thousands of years and rested in the brain, perhaps slowly decaying, until a certain point in human evolution, when it burst forth as a composite beast believed by those who claimed to behold it, or to do battle with it, to be very real and very dangerous.

Locating the lair of the brain-dragon requires a brief aside to review the structure of the human brain. Brain specialist Paul MacLean (cited in Laughlin, McManus, and d'Aquili 1992, 70–71) offers a simplified (but adequate for our purposes) model of the brain by dividing the human nervous system into three evolutionary strata: the new mammalian (telencephalon or neocortical structures), the paleomammalian (rhinencephalon or limbic system), and the reptilian (including the upper spinal cord, portions of the mesencephalon or midbrain, the diencephalon or thalamus–hypothalamus, and the basal ganglia). Laughlin explains,

> The organization of the reptilian brain has changed little in the higher animals. In humans this part of the nervous system mediates archaic regulatory functions such as metabolism, digestion, respiration, and the like. The limbic structures were added to the reptilian brain roughly a hundred million years ago to form the primitive mammalian brain, and their models mediate activities such as procreation, eating, searching, fighting, fear, joy, self defense, drinking, terror, foreboding, empathy, and hormonal regulation.

The brain-dragon rests then in the limbic structures of the brain. Marks (1987) more specifically pinpoints the parameters of the dragon's lair: "Mammalian deep structures that mediate certain components of fear and other defensive behaviors include the dentate and interposital nuclei of the cerebellum, locus ceruleus and median raphe nuclei, hypothalamus, septum, hippocampus, amygdala, cingulum, and thalamus" (222).

In this chapter I have outlined the basis of the dragon in space and time and how it became the composite creature that it is today. In briefly addressing the issue of animal phobias, we have seen how the brain-dragon continues to exert its influence on hundreds of thousands of phobia victims worldwide. The biocultural hypothesis concerning the dragon might offer an insight to the psychotherapists' quandary concerning the origin and nature of most animal phobias.

However, many details of the story of the world-dragon remain to be addressed. Why are dragons routinely described as having fiery, toxic breath? Why do dragons often have horns? Why are dragons associated with deep pools or wells? Why does the dragon basically look like a giant variation on a serpent or saurian? Why does the dragon roar? Why do many dragons have beards? Why are dragons so notoriously unfriendly to young women?

WHY DRAGONS
BREATHE FIRE

rhe preceding discussion proposed the basis for understanding the world-dragon as the result of a long history of natural selection in primate populations as they confronted the three basic primate predators. There is much more to the dragon, however, than the conventional image of the gigantic, flight-capable, snake- or saurian-like, clawed, and many-toothed beast. The details strongly suggest that the world-dragon is not merely the result of the fortuitous viewing of dinosaur fossils; these particulars—the beards, the horns, the fiery breath, the living in deep pools, the danger to women—could not be apparent in any way from viewing even the best preserved and most discernible dinosaur remains.

Natural selection theory will once more prove useful in explaining how the details of dragon form and behavior were shaped in the human brain. It will aid in understanding exactly how these details came to be in terms of the evolution of defensive behavior in primates.

First the obvious: the dragon is almost always implacably hostile and violent toward humans. Specific dragons are depicted as friendly and benign (as witness Puff the Magic Dragon, faery dragons), but this is a modern reading, or one that is used by an artist to create dramatic contrast, like "the gentle giant." Also, in cases where the dragon has come to be a symbol of state, it will be viewed as hostile only to enemies of the state. In the majority of cases, however, the dragon, like the primate predators, is dangerous and deadly.

A prey species tends to react to signals indicating the danger of the predator from a particular point of view or perspective. Note that the experiments with baby geese and ducks and with the lemurs at the Duke Center, in which a black silhouette of a hawk was hung above the subject animals, clearly assumed that the point of view of the observed animals was from the ground upward. Conversely, the various experiments with monkeys and infants in which snakes or models of snakes were introduced into a test situation suggested a perspective from above, looking down.

The Duke Center experiments, as well as the various field studies cited earlier, point out that primates react to the presence of predators when the potential threat is still some distance away. Obviously though, the most intense moment in this ancient engagement is the instant when the predator is attacking at close range. Seeing a big cat at a distance of a hundred yards and climbing a tree is clearly less crucial for survival than standing face-to-face with an attacker. That is, a wider parameter of efficient behavior exists in the former than in the latter. A monkey who responds slowly, but still within the parameters of safety, to the approach of a leopard will be in company with others of its group that may respond sooner, or with greater or lesser anxiety behavior.

THE DRAGON'S FACE

The most intense instant of the life-and-death encounter with the predator is the moment it attacks. The attack of the cat, the swooping eagle, or the striking snake is generally going to be a matter of ambush or surprise. At that instant, responses of less than a fraction of a second determine the difference between life and death. Therefore, many signals in the face of a charging predator, any one of which can ignite appropriate motion, will save life and perpetuate the genetic materials at least partially responsible for the continued existence of the prey. The most crucial signals of possible annihilation in the world of the ancient primates are premised upon the attacker being most often directly in front of the prey, staring it in the face: if some trigger or signal in the face of the attacker does not stimulate the potential victim to move quickly and appropriately, the animal will perish.

Another element in understanding how the ancient ancestral primate's point of view could affect how the brain-dragon came to be what it is involves the dimensions of the biologically triggered recognition of a dangerous predator. The signals, or triggering effects of the predator that move the prey to escape quickly, appear to be of a two-dimensional or flat, as opposed to a three-dimensional, nature. This is related to the reaction time of the prey to the attack or presence of the predator. If depth were part of the picture that the brain would have to recognize before the appropriate signals were sent to the body to facilitate escape, the ancestral primate would have taken longer to process; that is, it would not respond until the entire body of the predator was viewed and analyzed. The reaction time would be extended, thus reducing the survival potential for those who had to wait to see the entire animal as opposed to those ancient primates who could react to signals of danger immediately in front of them and from signals found in only two dimensions.

The flat perspective further suggests that the face and the extended appendages are the leading edge of the attack. One would assume this is probably true of any animal; the focus on the face to obtain information is no doubt more than merely a primate trait. It would be universal in animals that have faces.

The leading edge of the attack of a raptor is neither the beak nor the wings, but rather the extended taloned feet. Carnivores typically attack with their mouths, using appendages for running or springing at the prey, and in the case of cats, holding the prey while the mouth kills it. Snakes likewise lead with the mouth to inject venom, crush, and puncture, or in the case of constrictors, to acquire a purchase with the mouth while the coils wrap the prey in their suffocating embrace. The face and the leading appendages should be the dominant areas of predator recognition among primates, and should therefore be major aspects of the dragon's appearance and image.

It can be seen from the survey of the world-dragon (dragon images in a representative sample of world cultures) that the features of the dragon as they are revealed in art and myth worldwide seem to be the result of the "long distance" senses—seeing, hearing, smelling—as opposed to the "contact" senses such as taste and touch. Further, when the contact senses come into play, the assumption is that the dragon is already dead. Clearly the signals revealing the ancient struggle in the primate world between them and their hunters assume that confrontation is not a safe option; escape, when there is still lack of contact between predator and prey, is the desired goal.

The contact senses, touch and taste, are associated with power, while the long-distance senses suggest absence of power. The potential victims of the dragon will react to the sight of the beast or its smell or its roar, whereas the dragon-slaying culture hero experiences physical contact, touching the dragon as he wages his ultimately victorious battle. He then often drinks the blood of the dragon—that is, tastes it—to acquire various supernatural powers, a plot motif of many dragon tales worldwide. It is probably the case that the contact senses are more ancient in evolutionary terms than the long-distance senses.

The dragon found in cultural materials resulted from a biologically innate projection, which is filtered through the artistic norms of a particular culture. The sensibilities of the storyteller or artist must remain within universally recognized parameters for the viewers or the listeners to understand that they are being shown or told about a dragon. The form and traits of the world-dragon, the culturally manifested dragon, may suggest something about the history of the brain-dragon.

THE SCALED BODY

From the perspective of the primate, what is the major visual thrust of the dragon's presence? From dragon images worldwide, the most obvious trait is that the creature is reptilian. In terms of sheer mass of information, here equated to the mass of the image, that is the largest display of visual information. The scales and serpentine body are predominant, whereas the wings and carnivorous mouth occupy proportionally less "space" in the image. Why should this be if the preceding has suggested that three, not one, predators have formed the cultural dragon?

Perhaps the historical sequence of the appearance of the predators of the ancient primate might offer a clue. As was seen in chapter 4, reptiles evolved long before raptors and cats, so that ancestral primates had millions of years more experience with them. Maybe the predominantly reptilian body characteristics of the dragon image reflect the length of time the primates were being attacked by a particular predator and therefore undergoing selective stress. Those ancestral primates who could perceive and react to reptilian attackers more quickly and successfully would be favored over their slower kinsmen. That many of the large snakes are constrictors, using their bodies to crush and suffocate their victims, is yet another reason for the body of the serpent being a featured aspect of the dragon image.

Sue Parker and Kathleen Gibson (1979, 380 ff.) discuss the idea of "terminal addition" to explain the evolution of intelligence and cognitive abilities in our ancient ancestors. This concept is set within comments concerning ontogeny, the development of an individual organism; phylogeny, the evolution of a genetically related group; and the recapitulation hypothesis, which suggests that the ontogeny of the individual resembles the evolution of the group to which it genetically belongs. Parker and Gibson preface their comments on "terminal addition," using this quote from Steven S. Gould's *Ontogeny and Phylogeny* (1977): "Evolution occurs when ontogeny is altered in one of two ways: When new characters are introduced at any state of development . . . or when characters already present undergo changes in developmental timing" (4). Parker and Gibson continue, "Recapitulation is the repetition of the stages of phylogeny during ontogeny. Recapitulation is due to two processes: the first process is the extension of ancestral ontogeny, involving 'terminal addition' of new features at the end of ancestral ontogenies; the second process is the acceleration of the development of the new features" (380). Gould adds the very important observation that terminal addition is a product of natural selection.

What this suggests is a kind of layering effect of genetically based cognitive abilities through natural selection over vast ranges of time. The most ancient primate predator battle, that of the snake versus the ancestral primate, has been enhanced by the "terminal addition" effect of the recognition of the succeeding evolution of raptors and tree-climbing carnivores. Thus, the image of the dragon becomes a reptile with wings and a carnivore's mouth, a reflection through artistic images, perhaps, of the amount of time the primates have been dealing with the snake, the raptor, and the tree-climbing carnivore. The dragon image may be read as a kind of clock, or a temporal map of an important aspect of the history of primate predator/prey relations.

LARGE SIZE

The large size of the dragon is also understandable from the perspective of natural selection theory. Though small dragons are depicted—the basilisk is a famous example—the overwhelming majority of dragons are much larger than their human antagonists. If the basilisk's size is based on its potential for destruction, then it too would be "larger" than humans who might confront it, a creature who though only a few feet high is so deadly that merely seeing it brings death to the viewer. Cases of dragons of cosmic proportions, world-girdling beasts, also exist. But they, like the diminutive basilisk, are rare relative to the majority of dragon accounts. "Big," "potent," "powerful" can be communicated in a number of ways not necessarily related to physical dimensions.

The relative size relationship between humans and the dragon described in cultural art and lore is noteworthy. The size of the dragon relative to the culture hero who often confronts it is comparable to the size relationship between ancestral primates and raptors, big cats, and large snakes. Dragon combats, or encounters, scanned in a number of pictures and tales reveal that the human is on average about a fifth the size of the dragon. The size of the human relative to that of the dragon compares to that of the ancestral primate and its major predators.

There does seem to be variation in the size of the dragon depending upon whether the image is described in language or depicted in some visual art form. In folk tradition, one hears of the Japanese Dragon of Koshi, which was large enough to drape its body over eight hills and valleys; the Chinese Chien-Tang dragon, which measured nine hundred feet in length; or the various world-girdling dragons such as the biblical Leviathan, the Greek monster Typhon, with its wingspan of several hundred leagues, and the Norse creature the Midgard Serpent. In paintings, however, dragons are typically depicted in smaller sizes, both to meet the demands of the artistic medium being used and to display the dragon slayer, the culture hero, at work. It would be impossible in the Japanese case, for example, both to focus the picture on the hero, Susa-no-ow, and to depict the Dragon of Koshi in its hill-straddling splendor. If the Dragon of Koshi were depicted visually as the oral tradition describes him, it would be impossible even to see Susa-no-ow, except as a human figure about the size of the Koshi dragon's toenail. The dragons of oral tradition probably best represent the most ancient ideas about the beast, whereas more modern modes of presentation (painting, ceramic design, and so on) and more contemporary concerns (culture heroes and the rise of the state or new religions) are relatively more recent in appearance.

SPOTS AND CIRCLES

One design feature of the dragon's hide appears as a motif suggesting spots or circles. These are seen in the tale of Saint George's confrontation with the dragon in Libya, among other places. Before me now are images of dragons from Europe dating to the Middle Ages, from the Han period in China, and from an etching on a piece of pottery taken from a burial among the prehistoric peoples of the southeastern United States. All show patterns of spots and circles that, in relationship to each other and to the general size of the beast, resemble the spotted patterns of leopards, ocelots, and jaguars. These tree-climbing big cats, with their unique habit of caching game kills in trees, haunted the world of the ancestral primates.

A number of studies demonstrate that infants and monkeys often show fear of staring eyes, and one might suggest that the spots on the dragon are related. The circles and spots on dragons should not be interpreted as eyes because they are found all over the body of the dragon. When one finds animals with markings suggesting large eyes to a predator, as in various types of Amazonian moths and several varieties of butterflies, the spots will be large, clearly two in number, and set basically where a face might be expected.

Roaring

The dragon makes a lot of noise; its roar terrifies. But why should a dragon roar? The answer lies in the behavior of the primate predators. All of them make an explosive noise at the instant of attack, probably due to the rapid constriction of the body muscles that propel their spring or strike, forcing air from the mouth opening and resulting in a loud and frightening noise. Again, if one keeps in mind the relative perspective of the predator to the ancient primal ancestors of humans, the noise of the predator is very intense. Further, a sharp noise at the moment of attack momentarily freezes the prey, providing an additional advantage to the predator. In Asian martial arts, a loud shout (*ki-ai* in Japanese) is often issued at the moment of the attack. This focuses the energy of the attacker and allows him to expel air at the moment of the strike. Loud noises also irritate the inner ear, causing a momentary disturbance in muscle tone and balance, two elements of the physical system that must be in peak operation if the potential victim is to quickly respond and have a chance to escape the dangerous confrontation alive.

The sound of the attacking raptor can be of a slightly different order. One evening while fishing along the shores of a Florida lake, I witnessed a hawk attacking a gray dove, a strike that took place about fifty feet directly above me. I clearly heard a sonic shrill as the hawk dropped on its prey. The hair on the back of my neck rose as the sound froze the dove an instant before the hawk struck. Raptors also have very impressive shrieks, which would be amplified from the perspective of a small primate in dangerously close proximity.

The Feet

Dragons have interesting feet, one of the contributions of the raptor to the world-dragon (fig. 18). Talons are the killing points of the raptor, and they are presented to the prey at the instant of impending death, not the teeth, beak, or body. The dragons' feet are structured in a raptorial mode, with the claws on the toes typically longer and thinner than the blunt claws of animals such as turtles, alligators, and crocodiles. In the pre-

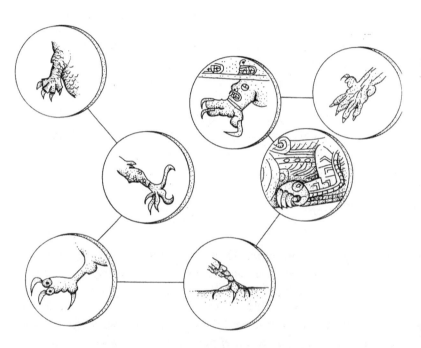

FIGURE 18:INTERESTINGLY ENOUGH, THE FEET OF THE WORLD-DRAGON DOES NOT TYPICALLY SHOW A FELINE PAW, BUT RATHER, SEPARATED TOES AND LONG CURVING NEEDLE TIPS—TALONS.

viously presented example of a Han dynasty dragon of China, for example, the right foreleg is depicted with toes and sharp talonesque claws, while the left foreleg has the paw or padded foot of the cat.

The killing signal of the raptor to which an ancient primate had to react, in that it was the last image he may have had, was two reaching taloned feet with a beak behind them and wings behind the beak. If the dragon's image derived ultimately from collapsing the signals or triggers of the three predators, the forefeet of the raptor apparently became one of the most prominent of these.

Most often the two leading legs of the four-legged dragon, the most typical arrangement, are the most active and dangerous, whereas the back two legs support the body or propel it forward but do not kill. The dragon's feet would not be pawed or padded like cats' feet, but rather would have separated toes and long, needle-pointed talons. A sensitivity to the look of two separated talon-toed feet rushing at the body would have to be precise.

The Hydra Effect

Most dragons are conventional beasts in that they have two or four legs, a set of wings, one head, and one tail; however, some dragons are hydras, or multi-appendaged beasts (fig. 19). The classic hydra of Greece has a number of heads emanating from the same neck. This type of dragon, found in many parts of the world, suggests a principle of design developed in relationship to the ancient primate's struggle with its predators. We can see in conventional cartooning and certain modern artistic movements (such as the Italian futurists, with their emphasis of depicting motion in two dimensions [Huneker 1915, 262 ff.] or in Marcel Duchamp's famous painting *Nude Descending a Staircase*) the replication of a particular piece of an image to convey motion. An ancient example of this technique is engraved on a bow found at Teyjat in southern France and dating between 30,000 and 10,000 B.C. (Fig. 20). The author of the book (1955) in which the engraving appears, Erwin O. Christensen, describes the image as a "herd of reindeer." This is not a likely interpretation because reindeer do not move en masse in straight lines. The draw-

FIGURE 19: THE GREEK HYDRA. THE MANY APPENDAGES APPEAR TO SUGGEST
MOVEMENT WITHIN THE IMAGE.

ing immediately below the "herd of reindeer" in Christensen's book, and described as a painting from the Altamira site in Spain, shows a crowded band of large mammals, a much more persuasive image of a herd than the curious drawing above it. There, the reindeer stands outlined on the left. Eighty to ninety slightly vertical strokes from left to right suggest outlines of the reindeer's rack riding above them. Finally, at the end of the visual scan, a complete reindeer is once again presented on the right. The effect perhaps was to depict the motion of a reindeer.

Paolo Graziosi (1960, pl. 89) presents another example from the same historical era, the Magdalenian, which might suggest motion. A horse stands on the left (fig. 21). The ancient artist has placed dozens of small vertical strokes side by side from right to left, with a bare suggestion of the outline of a horse's head above the strokes. As in the reindeer engraving described above, the last figure in the horse sequence is rendered with a full-body view. Once again, reindeer and horses do not arrange themselves in straight lines, and the ancient hunters would have known that very well. They did paint, engrave, and draw many convincing images of herds of the animals they hunted, with the tumult and chaos that such a scene would provoke, but the animals unnaturally presented in straight-line groupings were, I feel, about something else—motion. Analogies from other artistic traditions, noted above, suggest the possibililty of such an interpretation.

Moving predators are always more attention-grabbing than stationary ones. Note that some dangers do not move: quicksand, deep holes, cliffs, and boiling hot springs. Movement is a crucial feature in the fear of snakes. The writhing motion is particularly upsetting, as is the fluttering of feathers to many bird phobics. The hydra effect found in dragons with many legs or multiple wings says, "It moves," and the typical replicating of the head as part of the predator information suggests that the head is the most dangerous moving part of the predator. The many replicated images of head (mouth, teeth, eyes), legs, and wings might be seen as a recognition of the dangers of predator movement. The hydra effect could also mean "very much," a kind of exclamation, though the argument regarding motion is more to the point.

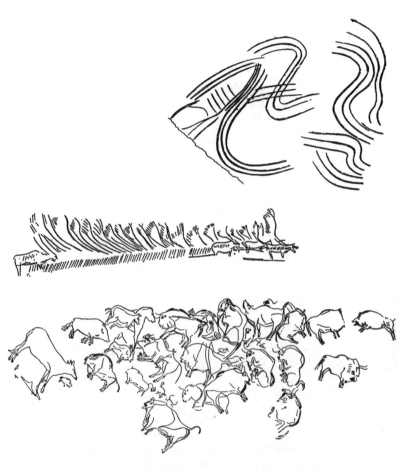

Figure 20: THE HERD OF REINDEER DEPICTED IN THE MIDDLE IMAGE FROM THE TEYJAT SITE IN SOUTHERN FRANCE SUGGESTS A DEPICTION OF THE MOVEMENT OF A SINGLE ANIMAL, WHEREAS THE LOWER IMAGE FROM THE ALTAMIRA SITE IN SPAIN OFFERS A MORE REALISTIC IMAGE OF HERDING ANIMALS.

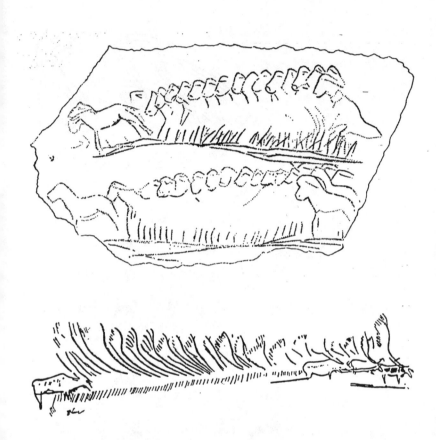

Figure 21: THE HORSES FROM THE CHAFFAUD SITE SHOW THE STYLE OF DEPICTION FOUND IN THE REINDEER IMAGE FROM TEYJAT. BOTH SUGGEST MOVEMENT.

HORNS

The hydra effect, the stylization of motion, might also explain several other features of the world-dragon: horns, crests, crowns, and beards. Two factors here could suggest a shape that would portray the dragon with horns or prominences on the head. Both of these possibilities arise from the flat perspective of the face of the predator, a cat in this instance. First, the ears of the cat stand erect from the top of its head, whereas the ears of most primates protrude from the sides of their heads. So a rushing animal that would be identified as alien to the ancestral primates would feature a face with two or more protuberances on the top of the head. This image indicated that something was very wrong and very dangerous about the creature rapidly approaching. Likewise, when a cat moves in for the attack, its tail generally stands upright with a slight curl at the tip. The tail poised in this way probably aids in balance. As the primal ancestor looked into the face of the cat during an attack, he would have seen the tip of the tail projecting from behind the head. Again, seen in a flat perspective, the tail would seem to arise from the top of the attacker's head. But if a cat has only one tail and dragons generally have two horns, and pronged horns at that, how can the cat be the ancient model?

The characteristic shape of the dragon's horns supports the flat perspective of a big cat's flickering tail. Dragon horns do not suggest the pointed tangs of the buck or caribou or the massive thickness of the moose's rack or the straight, pointed horns of various antelopes. Rather they generally appear as slightly blunted and rounded at the tip—like the tail of a big cat. The multiplicity of horns is related to the hydra effect. The cat's tail twitches nervously as it carries out its attack.

CROWNS

Dragons sometimes are described as wearing crowns (fig. 22). In some instances of the imaging of the dragon, no clear attempt has been made to set two horns on its head, but rather stylistic protuberances (points, crests, or "crowns"), which I propose are derived from the same reality. Further, hornlike protuberances on a variety of dragon images do not

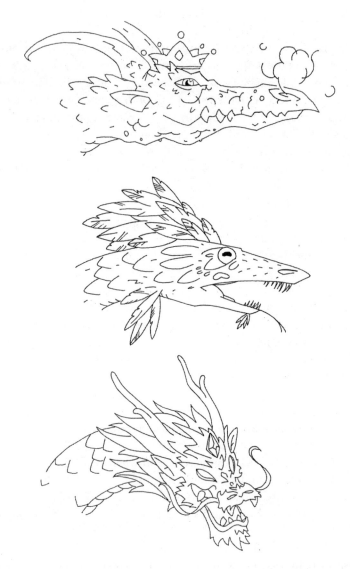

FIGURE 22: DRAGONS ARE ROUTINELY DEPICTED AS POSSESSING CRESTS, HORNS, CROWNS, OR FEATHERED PROTUBERANCES AROUND THE HEAD. THE AUTHOR SUGGESTS THAT THIS FEATURE, FOUND IN DRAGONS WORLDWIDE, IS ABOUT MOVEMENT.

seem to be clearly horns or crowns, but simply stylistic or balancing devices for the artist. The viewer does not rebel against this added touch because it echoes the flickering tail of the attacking carnivore behind the head of the face-forward attacker, an image set deeply in the brain.

Beards

The dragon's beard probably reflects the beards of the big cats. The chin hair of cats is of a stiff texture and projects outward, while their pelt lies flat to the body, is often slightly longer, and is sometimes of a different color than the chin beard. Female African lions, for example, have distinctive white chin beards. But the dragons' beards are relatively longer than those of the big cats. Why? Again, I think that depiction of motion has something to do with it. The beard of the female lion is a fourth or less the length of the face of the cat, whereas dragon beards are usually as long as or longer than the face. It has to do with the movement of the attacking animal—the cat in this instance. Imagine the perspective of the cat's face looming toward you, and understand that the cat will rock its head up and down, positioning itself to sink its teeth into you. And though you may not be focusing on the beard, the beard is there and would appear to be longer. The model of time-lapse photography is useful. If one photographed a lion's face at the moment of attack using this method, the chin beard would be simultaneously both higher and lower than its central positioning, resulting in a mental image of a longer beard, as is usual in the depiction of dragons.

Culture obviously plays a major role in which features of the dragon will be accentuated under various circumstances. Cultural ideas about senior males with beards, or beards as indicative of experience, religious status, or leadership, would be assured in such a culture's rendering of a bearded dragon, whereas in a culture where human beards have no symbolic significance, the beard of the dragon may or may not be shown or described. In a world where deer hunting is of key importance, horns suggested by the brain-dragon may be exaggerated, but they may be very minimal features in a culture that does not hunt or depend upon horned or antlered animals.

Deadly Breath

The dragon's breath is uniformly commented upon and is always noxious, hot, fiery, smoky, and/or poisonous. Again consider the attack of the cats. The breath of the attacking animal will be hot and reeking of putrid animal meat, particularly from the perspective of arboreal vegetarians. Thus, the breath of the attacker is connected with danger. The smoky look of the dragon's breath might be related to the condensation of the carnivore's hot breath being expelled into the relatively cool air of the early morning or evening when the big cats hunt.

"Immediate danger," however, is the major signal of the breath. In a very few cases, the dragon issues floods of water from its mouth—not smoke and fire but definitely dangerous in that these expulsions generally are connected with deadly floods.

Water

This naturally leads to a possible explanation of dragons being almost universally associated with water, especially deep pools and wells. "Dragon wells" are found in native North America in the lore that tells the Cherokee of the Southeast that the *uktena* lives in deep pools far back in the mountains and informs the Hopi of the Southwest that Pululukon lives in deep springs and wells. "Dragon wells" are found in China, Ireland, Scotland, Egypt, Yucatan, Hawaii, and in the vacinity of Jerusalem, to name but a few locations. Our most ancient association with the dragon places it in water. When cultures became horticultural, with an accelerated interest in rain, the dragon's connection with water expanded to include the rain, since dragons also live in the air or come from the sky.

Why, however, would the dragon be associated with water? The answer lies in the dangers of the water hole. As noted earlier, the transformation of the arboreal primates into the terrestrial forms that gave rise to humans occurred when the earth's primal forest cover was in places ravished by drying climatic conditions, forming a mixed forest and savanna habitat. The arboreal creatures, though they could obtain water from rain puddles and notches and holes in trees, found that in dry seasons this form of easy water evaporated. They were forced to the ground to locate water holes.

At these holes predators were provided with abundant prey that were compelled into the open and, in the case of the primate, had to bow their heads with their eyes facing downward to drink. The snake often lived in association with the water, cats hunted by the water holes, and raptors watched from their perches as small game came to drink. The raptors could hunt on the edges of water holes without the problems inherent in picking monkeys out of the branches of dense tree cover. Approaching the pool of water would become for the ancient primates an activity fraught with feelings of danger. T. T. Struhsaker and J. S. Gartlan (cited in Bramblett 1976, 137) note that "the severity of the dry season in the Cameroons leads to concentration of patas monkey troops around permanent water holes, with an increased frequency of antagonistic encounters."

Eyes

The wide and staring eyes of the dragon are distinguished in folklore as possessing the power to paralyze victims. In many European languages the word for "dragon" suggests penetrating gazes or sharp-sightedness. In paintings of dragons worldwide, the eyes are most typically wide open, bright, fiery, and large. During attacks, predators' eyes remain in very close proximity to their prey and are, in the case of our three major predators, wide open. This serves two purposes: to help the predator gauge distance and to momentarily freeze the prey, as would a loud noise.

Young Women and Dragons

Another very typical dragon-lore plot element worldwide is the antagonism between dragons and women of prime childbearing years. It is significant that dragons rarely bother postmenopausal women or prepubescent females. It is the young maiden who repeatedly appears as the special target of dragon harassment. One way of understanding this theme is to appreciate the different level of investment or cost between males and females in terms of perpetuating the genetic heritage of the group to which they belong. Edward O. Wilson (1978) writes,

> The human egg is eighty-five thousand times larger than the human sperm. The consequences of this gametic dimorphism ramify throughout the biology and psychology of human sex. The most important immediate result is that the female places a greater investment in each of her sex cells. A woman can expect to produce only about four hundred eggs in her lifetime. Of these a maximum of about twenty can be converted into healthy infants. The costs of bringing an infant to term and caring for it afterwards are relatively enormous. In contrast, a man releases one hundred million sperm with each ejaculation. Once he has achieved fertilization his purely physical commitment has ended. His genes will benefit equally with those of the female, but his investment will be far less. (124)

In terms of natural selection, females of childbearing years would exercise extreme caution toward predators as compared to other age and gender categories. The female with a newborn is the future of the group. Males, who could theoretically impregnate thousands of females in their lifetime, are genetically somewhat less valuable to the group's future. An attack against a female presents more danger for the group than an attack against a male. In primates, most crucial child care rests in the hands of females, who are hampered by juveniles and infants; thus behavior in females that creates a heightened sense of alertness to danger toward them and their offspring would be selected for. This is reflected in the particular sexual antagonism of the dragon toward females and in contemporary predator-related phobias in females.

All studies verify that females suffer as the major victims of agoraphobia, and though agoraphobia presents many manifestations, the fear of being alone in an open space is a recurring theme. The relationship of this sensitivity to the survival requirements of ancient primates has been noted earlier. It is related to the "wall-clinging" behavior of rats and mice, likewise an instinctual behavior selected for over time in rodent populations.

Most females develop the symptoms of this phobia between the ages of fifteen and thirty-five, prime childbearing years, and particularly high rates of phobic disorders exist among mothers. In 1975, a survey of over 1,000 agoraphobics at the Sparthfield Clinic at Rochdale in Lancashire, England, determined that 90 percent were mothers (cited in Melville 1977). Also noted was a significant tendency for children to report the same kind and number of fears as their mothers (Marks 1969, 170).

Perhaps more relevant to this discussion, the same picture reappears in animal phobias. The vast majority of animal phobics are females of childbearing age. Although animal phobias occur often in both sexes, the few that remain after puberty are mainly suffered by females. Girls showed significantly more fears than boys (50 percent vs. 36 percent).

TREASURES AND MAGIC JEWELS

Dragons are often portrayed as guardians of treasures. The dragon lore of both China and of the aborigines of the southeastern United States claims that if acquired by a culture hero, a gemstone or a pearl in the dragon's head can grant great powers. Even the Lapps of Finland have the tradition of the "snake stones," rare white rocks produced by snakes that can give the finder certain powers. The Lapp Johan Turi (1966) writes,

> He who finds one [snake-stone] will never be overcome by the law... ah, the man who could find one! First you must find the snakes' mating place, when they are pairing they cast a white stone here and there, and he who goes and watches in secret where they are casting the stone here and there, he must snatch the stone and run to water and if he reaches the water before the snakes, then he gets the stone, but if the snake gets there first, then it is dangerous. But the one who has made sure beforehand where the nearest water is, he reaches it first... the snakes have been hindered for a little, while they looked for the stone, and in the meantime the man has run to the water. And if he has the stone, then he is a law-cunning man all the days of his life. (147)

The "treasure guardian" aspect of the world-dragon may relate to the three primate predators' blocking or guarding. They protect the riches of trees' upper branches, the location of the most succulent leaves and flowers, which are the hunting zones of the raptors, and the riches of the ground (the source of roots, fruits, nuts, leaves, and insects), which is the hunting territory of snakes and carnivores. The jewel generally described in the head of the dragon can be understood as part of the more recent history of the dragon (as the association of dragons with rain among horticultural peoples), a generalization of the association of the predators with water holes.

Further, the shining, faceted gems obtained from dragons are not products of nature. Stone cutting and polishing is a cultural act perpetrated on a rare and valuable commodity. Pearls do not simply appear on the beach but must be acquired through direct human action, performing an operation on a pearl oyster.

It is the killing of the dragon that allows the culture hero to obtain the gem, the product of culture. This might be connected to the oft-repeated theme in world mythology of a hero or god performing an act by which he transcends his lower tendencies to become a cultured creature, sophisticated and advanced beyond the lower life forms. It may simply mean "beyond the past," "beyond nature," or "cultural" as opposed to "natural." Perhaps the jewel in the head relates to the often noted intelligence of dragons, permitting some of them even to converse with their attackers and victims.

The dragon is a composite of shapes, smells, and images that trigger defensive behavior, fear, or avoidance in primates. The various signals—like the diving shrill and shriek of the raptor attack and the vision of two sets of separated toes with talons attached—would select for those ancient primates that could perceive the true nature of these signals quickly. The signals of the attacking big cat that would enable the primate to escape would include any of the various physical traits or groupings of traits of the dragon (large eyes, horns, and roar). Maybe the same escape procedure would occur in an animal that might be genetically programmed to respond to a blast of hot air or "horns" above the head or wide open eyes, singly. Likewise, in the attack of the serpent, the body is most significant. Collapse these traits, and one finds all of these elements combined in one beast, the brain-dragon, and its cultural manifestation, the dragon of world art and mythology.

TIME OF THE
DRAGON SLAYERS

n interesting problem arises when one compares the presence of the cultural dragon with the basic models of sociopolitical organization recognized by most modern anthropologists. The brain-dragon, though built in to the human psyche through natural selection over millions of years, is surprisingly not universally manifested to the same extent in all forms of sociopolitical organizations. In some cases a real flesh-and-blood dragon haunts the landscape, while in others the dragon exists not as a real entity but as a symbol of the highest level of leadership and power. And sometimes the dragon lives only as a figure in various forms of entertainment or as an image in children's fairytales, and nothing more.

Heinz Mode is one of the few modern dragon commentators who recognizes the relationship between dragon fascination and types of social organization. In his discussion (1973) of various types of dragons found around the world he notes,

> It may have been noticed that no mention has been made of ancient America nor of ancient Africa, the South Seas and Australia. That these areas may in fact largely be left out of the account is due to a fact

already stated: namely that the idea of monsters arises at a relatively late stage in cultural development. . . . The observation that monsters were not created originally by the so-called "primitive" peoples, as one might have expected, but are in fact to a large extent the product of highly developed civilizations is surprising enough.(15)

I do not agree with Mode in his assertion that ancient America, Africa, the South Seas, and Australia "may, in fact, largely be left out of the account," as my discussion in the introduction concerning universal dragons indicates, but I do agree with his observation that the dragon seems to flourish more at later than at earlier stages of cultural evolution.

To sharpen the focus and provide some context for the succeeding discussion of cultural evolution, we might pause briefly to outline some of the ways anthropologists have sought to organize the tremendous variety of human sociocultural types found over the globe and through time. One of the earliest was to classify societies by their subsistence behavior (how they made a living) as hunter/gatherers, pastoralists, horticulturalists, or agriculturalists. It has generally been assumed that hunter/gatherers represented the earliest forms of society, and those focused on gardening and agriculture the most recent.

A current model is based on neoevolutionary cultural theory. It assumes that cultures evolve in relationship to their efficiency in harnessing power, and that power harnessing begins at the level of human organization—more succinctly, political organization. Hence, a model is put forward that suggests the evolutionary unfolding of less to more complex forms of sociopolitical organization. That this model is more than a historically based theory is seen in the fact that all forms of sociopolitical organization described by this school of anthropological thought continue to exist to this day.

Billions of human beings have walked the earth since the appearance of our line of humanity several million years ago in East Africa. During that immense span of time, the ancient human ancestors clustered themselves, much as modern-day primate troops still do, into groupings called bands. About 90 percent of all humans throughout time have lived in bands, typically small, nomadic or seminomadic hunting and gathering groups numbering between fifty and one hundred individuals.

Again, as with most nonhuman primate populations, the band is integrated on the basis of kinship, providing for its members the feeling of being one large family. Commonly band members refer to each other not by name but by kinship terms. Following from this, bands are usually exogamous; that is, they require their members to marry outside the band because to do otherwise would be incestuous.

Bands tend to be egalitarian groupings where all members, theoretically at least, have equal access to resources and prestige. Generally there is no concept of private ownership of property in band societies. Territory and food are communal resources, usually shared among members to some degree each day. Leadership in bands is noncoercive. Senior males with good records of citizenship and leadership are looked to for advice concerning camp movement, relations with other nearby groups, problems over the division of game animals, and interband disputes; however, the members of a band are free to ignore this counsel. Lacking such institutions as courts of law, police, and jails, bands must depend upon their ability to socialize their members to feelings of kinship and the qualities of generosity, kindness, compassion, and freedom from bad temper. Further, not only do bands continue to exist in various parts of the world, but the general nature of band living is still experienced even by modern Americans in the day-to-day pattern of family life, the contemporary remnant of band society in the modern world.

As food production—horticulture, pastoralism, agriculture—became more complex somewhere around 8,000 to 10,000 B.C., a new form of socio-political organization, the tribe, evolved where these modern forms of food production took hold. Tribes can also arise where natural food supplies are extraordinarily plentiful, as was the case with the Calusa of southwest Florida or the Nootka and Kwakiutl of the Northwest Coast culture area. Such conditions, however, are rare.

Tribes are collections of bands that usually speak the same language, follow the same methods of subsistence, consider themselves culturally similar if not identical, and operate in the same general territory. Tribes are integrated by institutions, such as clubs and clans, that cross-cut band membership, bonding the largely autonomous bands at a more complex level.

Tribes, in that they are comprised of a number of bands, can have large populations. Whereas American Indian tribes may have populations ranging from several hundred to several thousand, African tribes, such as the Nuer, have several hundred thousand members.

Bands generally form as tribes to defend themselves against enemies, attack enemies, or facilitate large-scale economic or political actions on a scale beyond the capabilities of bandsmen. Tribes are generally more sedentary than bands because of the necessity of controlling territories for Neolithic forms of food production: farming and herding. They show a fission/fusion characteristic with respect to constituent bands. Often tribes will organize in full array with all bands together, while at other times bands may split away from the tribal group and follow their own interests before regrouping at the tribal level. The Cheyenne Indians of the North American High Plains, for example, would come together as a tribe in the late spring, hunt bison and raid through the summer, and then split into band units as the winter closed in and game became scarce. Sometimes these band units would, as the winter deepened, disperse into family units. When good weather and game returned, the families would rendezvous to form bands, and the bands would reform as the Cheyenne tribe.

Leadership in tribes tends to follow the example of bands. Kinship is the basis of organization, and senior kinsmen in each band form its advisory board. Tribes usually operate through councils comprised of band representatives. As with the bands, decisions are noncoercive. A band that does not like a tribal decision is free to go its own way. Methods of leadership may rest on subtle, and not so subtle, economic and political pressures. The line between suggestion and force is therefore very fine in such societies.

As warfare evolved with the rise of sedentary and semisedentary food production, pastoral ranges, and village life about ten to twelve thousand years ago, a new type of sociopolitical organization, the chiefdom, rose. Chiefdoms possess certain features also found in the tribe. They both depend heavily on kinship as the basis of social organization and on gardening and herding for subsistence. However, something novel appears that separates the chiefdom from the tribe, namely the rise of permanent, centralized leadership, the position of the chief. This individual wields power, varying in degree from chiefdom to chiefdom, and coordinates economic, military, political, social, and religious activities. Chiefdoms, at the top of their organization, are no longer egalitarian. Leadership becomes an inherited position with the power to coerce or enforce decisions made by the chief. The ability of the chief to force a decision stems from the military context that often surrounds the evolution of the tribe to chiefdom.

Tribes generally have a peace chief/war chief type of organization. Certain members of the tribe routinely argue in tribal or band counsel discussions for the use of force through military action to solve various problems concerning external political relations, territory, trade, and such. These are the war chiefs. Peace chiefs, on the other hand, champion compromise and peaceful solutions to problems. If, however, a chronic state of warfare develops, the role of the war chief becomes entrenched and often inherited through the male line. It is through his position as military commander that the chief comes to power.

Regardless of the way the chief achieves his position, his presence means the potential for a greater degree of coordination of social units than was found at the tribal level of society. In chiefdoms, because of centralized control, we find the first appearance of full-time specialists, whereas previously all individuals, even if they were part-time healers or artisans, also had to see to their own subsistence. The chief thereby assists in increased productive levels. As centralized controller he gathers wealth from the population as taxation, usually in the form of offerings, donations, or ritual presentations, and redistributes this wealth in the areas of public works, military support, and so on. He takes a sizable cut for his troubles, which means that he and his family become wealthy relative to the general population. With real wealth and its connection to political power, the egalitarian world of the bands and tribes is transcended, and the way is paved for the later rise of states.

A chiefdom evolves into a primitive state, or kingdom, when the integration of the social group involves a monopoly of force both to protect the group against outsiders and to control the home population. Warfare was the condition that set certain African chiefdoms, such as the Zulu and Ashanti, on the road to becoming primitive states. As the primitive state becomes organized by law, as opposed to the whims of its hereditary leadership, the form of the modern state is approached. We do not need to delineate the traits of the modern state at this point, as sufficient information has been presented to discuss the relationship between dragons and political groupings.

An additional method of organizing societies of the world for study by scholars is based on differentiating between uncentralized and centralized political systems. Bands and tribes are uncentralized, in that the most important decisions are made in a democratic manner through group discussion where the comments of all ages and both genders may be taken into consideration in reaching a final resolution of some problem. In centralized political systems, decisions are made by a single individual, as in a chiefdom, or by a legally restricted and elite body of individuals, as in a state.

Using the above typologies, one can observe that dragons, considered as real creatures, enjoyed popularity at a point in history when the tribe was evolving into a chiefdom, or more broadly speaking, when an uncentralized political system was evolving into a centralized system. Prior to this time, surprisingly enough, dragons were not significant in everyday life or mythology, and after this time the dragon quickly domesticates and is reduced to first a symbol of political power and later to a mere fairy-tale element. Dragons are indeed found among band level societies. The dragons of the Australian aborigines and the Inuit, both classic band-type societies, evidence this. Likewise, a few cases of dragons are found in tribal societies.

Dragons become real and begin terrorizing villages and entering combat with culture heroes at the dawn of the primitive state, at a time when a particular society seems to have one foot planted in a tribal world of multiple bands and/or villages united under a loose tribal identity and the other in the embryonic centralized structure of chiefdoms or kingdoms. When the centralized organization has entered its earliest level of solidification, the dragon becomes a symbol of state, and its nature changes to reflect that fact. No longer the definition of savagery, it becomes civilized. No longer real, no longer conceived as a beast to be hunted and killed, it becomes a symbol of earthly power.

In this respect, it is instructive to compare the period in European history when dragon sightings reached their peak with an observation of the political situation. Though accounts speak of dragon combat as early as the eighth century, as in the saga of Beowulf in the British Isles, and the sixth century, in the case of the French dragon the *gargouille,* the peak of Europe's fascination with the living, breathing dragon seems to fall between the eleventh and thirteenth centuries, during the European medieval period. By widening the temporal parameters to include a period roughly from A.D. 500 to A.D. 1500, we witness a time of major growth and development in many parts of the world, a time when the roots of the modern nations of the world were being formed, a time of the dragon. The Middle Ages in the history of Western Europe are often divided into the Early Middle Ages ("the Dark Ages"), a period of disorder and decline between the fifth and tenth centuries, and the High Middle Ages, dated from the eleventh to the fourteenth centuries, a time of rapid advance toward a more modern and centralized form of state government.

In the mid-eleventh century, Byzantine culture was spreading north through trade and warfare to Christianize the Slavic peoples. After A.D. 911, the Russian city of Kiev became a major trade link between Asia and Europe, and Moscow rose as the "Third Rome" in the mid-fifteenth century. On the Arabian Peninsula in A.D. 610, Muhammad, a businessman in Mecca, had a religious vision from which derived the religion of Islam. Within several hundred years Islam came to dominate much of the known world, preserving Greek art and philosophy and advancing the arts, literature, and architecture, as well as setting much of the basis of modern mathematics, astronomy, geometry, and medicine.

Europe, relative to the energetic history of Islam and the Byzantine cultures, lagged behind in developing of the roots of nationhood. Charles the Great (Charlemagne), king of the Franks, united much of Europe in the mid-ninth century. After his death, however, this union unraveled because of internal struggles as well as foreign invasion. The feudal system resulted in succeeding ages of conflict. It was based in the need for protection from raiding Moors, Vikings, and Magyars, a people of central Asia who raided into Europe from bases in modern-day Hungary. The vassal pledged loyalty to the lord, who in turn provided protection and expected in return payment in the form of taxes and periods of military service. The important point is that each unit possessed its own set of laws and gave no allegiance to a central government. Even though the position of kingship was present at this time, medieval kings were notoriously weak rulers, usually mere figureheads. When they did exist, they were easily controlled by a collection of lords who lived self-sustaining lives on their great manors.

However, around A.D. 1000 the European economy began to grow. New farming techniques increased food supplies. Trade expanded as the knights of the manors gained control of lawless elements in the population. Markets flourished. Towns were established along trading routes. A money economy was born that ultimately led to the rise of a new merchant class and the fall of feudalism. Wealth meant more taxation, which also led to the rise of truly powerful kings.

In A.D. 1215 the Magna Carta placed some legal limits on the growing power of the English king. In France the monarchies were flexing their muscles under Philip II, Louis IX, and Philip IV. To use terminology introduced earlier, the period of the dragon, from the eight century to the thirteenth century, saw a move in European history from the multicentric polities of groups of constantly squabbling feudal warlords to the later rise of unicentric authorities, kingship, the immediate precondition of the modern state.

That the peak of dragon excitement in Europe seems to correlate in some way with the shift from the Early to the High Middle Ages is clear, but why this happened is not. A few points may suggest a tentative solution. First, the shift from a multicentric type of society to a more unicentric one, from a collection of loosely organized villages and manors to a modern state, happened fairly rapidly because it was often accomplished by military means. The end of noble family lines, control of territory, and political ascendancy could be accomplished with a few sword cuts delivered in a matter of seconds. However, if the death of some noble occurred because a king was attempting to solidify central authority, a typical scenario in the Middle Ages, the vassals of that downed knight would experience a major shift and dislocation of their life fabric. Second, such rapid social change tends to upset societies, typically leading to the rise of new religions, warfare, and a concomitant increase in psychopathology, social violence, crime, and drug and alcohol addiction—classic signals of social stress.

Anthropologist Anthony F. C. Wallace provided some useful concepts in his discussion (1970, 188–99) of the manner in which people construct new religions, "revitalization movements" in his terminology, to cope with crisis. The central motivating force leading to the creation of revitalization movements is a collectively perceived disruption in what Wallace calls the "mazeway."

The mazeway is the individual's perception of the world around him. It encompasses everything from assumptions about the way the natural world should act to understanding and acceptance of the nature and functioning of the sociocultural domains, acceptance of traditional values, religion, and philosophy, and self-concept at the level of mind, body, and spirit. In a period of relative equilibrium, changes in the mazeway occur slowly and in such a way that the individual can integrate these changes without stress or anxiety. However, when external changes in the mazeway interfere with the integration and dynamics of life for a substantial number of people, disillusionment with the previous mazeway sets in. Those affected will experience fear, panic, anxiety, shame, guilt, depression, or apathy—deep and primal emotions residing in the vicinity of the brain-dragon. Perhaps the powerful conflicts that occur when a significant percentage of a population experiences mazeway dislocation touch the same emotional strata occupied by the brain-dragon. Maybe the dragon manifests as a means of attacking the fear and uncertainty that may arise from rapid social change, particularly such a fundamental change as that from multicentric authorities to unicentric authority, or more dramatically from the band/tribe to the chiefdom/kingdom/state.

In a more technical vein, these rapid social changes could have overloaded the hippocampus of those who were swept up in the dragon-hysteria. The circuitry connecting the cortex and hippocampus (cortico-hippocampal loops) is responsible for novelty detection and memory storage. The hippocampus could be the "gateway" to the ancient memories stored in the cortex, memories triggered by the "novelty overload" of the times.

To attack and destroy the dragon may be a prerequisite of this state of cultural evolution. It is significant to note that the tale of the European dragon is always presented ultimately to highlight the dragon slayer. This dragon slayer generally succeeds because he represents a pan-European

Christian religion or a newly emerging state. Disruptive changes in both religion and political organization greatly, and negatively, shift the mazeways of those buffeted by the changes, those attacked by the dragon. They are in turn saved by the agents of the new religious and/or political order, the dragon slayer. This act generally is a prelude to the realignment of the preceeding epoch's religious and political organization.

A faint echo of the relationship between a dragon and its slayer, and the resultant heroic opinion of the slayer, is found in a variety of contemporary cultural manifestations that connect the taming of serpents with spiritual advancement. In images of yoga and yogic heroes in India, cobras drape around the saint's neck, wrap around his waist, or coil at his feet. In the highest levels of a Pentacostal Holiness sect, most represented in West Virginia, handling rattlesnakes and copperheads without being bitten is a sign of Holy Ghost possession. Among the Hopi Indians of Arizona, a famous "rain dance" entails the members of the religious dance troop moving to a slow drumbeat as they hold live snakes in their teeth.

That the differences in the mazeway between the earlier multicentric forms and later unicentric forms are dramatic is easy to appreciate. In a band, for example, all members are family. In a state, family orientation becomes diminished in importance, and kinship increasingly fades before the functioning of the state. In a band, all have some say in leadership; in a state, only a few do. In a band, each member is equal and free, while in a state, people find themselves unequal in terms of wealth and power. Whereas slavery does not exist in bands, it finds its highest development in states. In a band, information flows freely. A state, on the other hand, must keep secrets from the people. In a band, all theoretically have access to wealth and scarce goods and resources, but in a state, access to wealth is strongly controlled by a few. Religious experience in bands is typically very individualistic, whereas state religions are generally monopolies run by a priestly caste. These are terrifying differences, profound in their denial of the premises of social life that have been part of the primate experience for millions of years. Paths burned into our consciousness by cultural and natural selection over millions of years are suddenly turned upside down. And what happens when people find that their most fundamental images of the world are crumbling? They often turn to religion. They become fascinated with the largest concepts of good and evil, and they arrange to perceive the good in the form of the culture hero, the god, and the evil in the form of an image their brains have been har boring as the most fundamental evil for hundreds of thousand of years—the dragon.

This magnitude of change reaches beyond the mere need to shift philosophical paradigms concerning the nature of religion, family, and politics to fit a new order of sociopolitical existence. We turn to Wallace (1970) again: "There is some reason to suspect that such dramatic resynthesis depends on a special biochemical milieu, accompanying the 'stage of exhaustion' of the stress syndrome, or on a similar milieu induced by drugs" (99). It is the biochemical dimension that summons the dragon to be confronted and hopefully destroyed by an agent of the new order.

Wallace's conception of mazeway disruption and resulting revitalization movements shares some common ground with the study of the behavior known as mass hysteria, or in more recent years, "collective exaggerated emotions." Sociologist John Farley (1998) describes "mass hysteria" this way: "Mass hysteria occurs when many people in a sizable geographic area perceive and respond frantically to some danger. Often the danger is not real or, if real, is not as great as people believe" (488).

Examining some of the beliefs that contemporary populations in the United States have entertained as "real" might help to explain the behavior of the thousands of individuals in the Middle Ages who reported seeing dragons, being attacked by dragons, or engaging in combat with dragons. In 1938, for example, CBS Radio carried a life broadcast of H. G. Wells's science fiction classic *The War of the Worlds*. In dramatic fashion, a program of dance music was suddenly interrupted by a news bulletin announcing that Martians had landed in New Jersey and were set on conquering the world. Even though the radio announcer stated before, during, and after the broadcast that the show was fiction, over a million Americans believed that Martians had landed and set about arming themselves, barricading their houses, hiding in storm cellars, or taking to the road in cars and trucks to escape the extraterrestrial attackers! A similar panic took place in Portugal in 1988 when *The War of the Worlds* was staged to celebrate the fiftieth anniversary of the original broadcast.

Farley's explanation of the panic associated with the famous radio broadcast reflects what I have been suggesting about the belief in dragons; that is, the setting of the panic event features deep anxiety felt by a large percentage of the population. "Part of the reason that this radio play about an invasion of hostile Martians led to mass hysteria was that the world was on the brink of World War II. People felt insecure and afraid; events seemed out of control" (1998, 488).

The theme of attack seems to permeate not only the dragon beliefs of the Middle Ages in Europe but also most modern occurrences of mass hysteria. During World War II, in the "Great Los Angeles Air Raid," sizable portions of the population of the city believed they were under attack by the Japanese. The panic gripped not only the civilians who poured reports of Japanese sightings into local police and newspaper phone lines, but also the military who manned and fired antiaircraft guns at phantom Japanese planes.

Sociologists Nehum Medalia and Otto Larson wrote (1958) about the "Seattle windshield pitting epidemic of 1954," which erupted in a town north of Seattle when local citizens reported tiny pits and bubbles in the windshields of their cars and trucks. Often this pitting was accompanied by the presence of minute metallic fragments seemingly embedded in the glass. Within a few weeks, police in Seattle had received reports of such damage to over three thousand vehicles. As the population sought an explanation for the pitting, the most common assumption related it to H-bomb testing in the Pacific. As the hysteria rose, the mayor of Seattle appealed to the governor of Washington and to the president of the United States on the evening of April 15 for emergency assistance. Soon after, the hysteria died away. A group of researchers later concluded that the windshields had always been pitted. No one had noticed it before because drivers generally look through the windshield, not at it. The anxiety level in the general population had generalized a threat that did not exist.

I remember a lecture about mass hysteria in Sociology 101 during my freshman year at college. The example was the case of the "Mad Gasser" of Sassoon, Wisconsin. As I recall, in the mid-1950s many of the citizens of Sassoon came to believe that they were under attack by a madman who would pump sleeping gas into their bedrooms at night through a small tube and then enter the homes for a variety of criminal activities on the property and inhabitants. After the hysteria had diminished, studies found that the "Mad Gasser" had never existed and related the event to local stresses in the population. From an earlier period in American history, the witch hysteria of Salem, Massachusetts, presents another example of a population perceiving itself to be under attack by nonexistent entities.

In almost all cases, the attack perceived in mass hysteria issues from the involved population's belief in an ultimate danger: Martians attacking the earth; Japanese attacking Los Angeles during World War II; H-bomb testing attacking automobiles; witches and "Mad Gassers" attacking the local citizens with Satanism, secret chemistry, and stealth. In the European Middle Ages, the dragon was the greatest danger that could be imagined. It was the H-bomb, the Martian attack, and the "Mad Gasser" all rolled into one.

It is not surprising then that the dragon was quickly associated with Satan, and the European dragon slayer was in almost all cases depicted as a Christian hero. The dragons tended to be local or provincial in nature, whereas the God of the Christians symbolized an order that transcended local concerns. The defeat of the dragon might be seen as the final severing of the local kinship-based social unit to make way for the nation-oriented social unit. The dragon seems to fade as a real force when kinship affiliations become less significant, a typical factor in the development of the state. Further, the Christian knights who slayed dragons to prove that the God of Christianity was more powerful than the minions of the devil also prepared the way for the rise of the state by acts that, though self-serving, ultimately laid the infrastructure upon which the European state could rise: formation of armies, maintenance of law and order, protection of travelers, consciousness of the rights of landowners, and building of large castles and fortifications that became the basis for almost all the cities of modern Europe.

One of the most efficient means of unifying a fragmented group is to present them with a common enemy. The dragon was an equal-opportunity destroyer, attacking civilized locations such as villages, farms, markets, and churches from zones of utmost mystery and strangeness to the European citizens of the Middle Ages. Dragons traditionally were said to sally forth from their lairs in the wildest mountains or the deepest forests, places that normal humans did not traverse. All villages, regardless of their connection to local patterns of feudal relationships, stood helpless before a common foe, and that foe came from environments generally alien to those living in the agricultural basis of Medieval European economies.

This situation replicates in modern times the relationship of the ancient arboreal primates to their predators. When not under attack by predators, the ancients, as suggested by the behavior of contemporary primate troops, behaved in individualistic ways: seeking food, mating, grooming, and so on. When the predator came, the group responded. Likewise, as the Europeans of the Middle Ages saw the source of the dragon as areas of extreme alienness to humans—dank caves, deep pools, wild mountain reaches, sea bottoms, haunted forests—the ancient primates would also "understand," as indicated by the patterned nature of their predator calls and responses, that the killer was coming from a zone alien to the arboreal primate ancestor—the sky and the dark forest floor.

Though having a dragon as a foil during a period when multicentric societies were being pushed toward acceptance of a unicentric form would be handy, the real source of the dragon is not the cynical manipulation of symbols to provide a means of unifying scattered polities, though this surely happened once the beast was loose in the public imagination. The question is, Why would the dragon suddenly erupt into public awareness even though its source, the brain-dragon, was present even prior to the evolution of modern *Homo sapiens,* though somehow dormant? The following comparisions to widely recognized innate behaviors may offer parallel examples.

Language learning abilities of children are a typical example of a behavior that is believed to be innate but which seems to activate at a predictable time in the growth of the child. In all societies, infants learn to speak at roughly the same age (between one and two years of age), in a relatively short time span, and at roughly the same speed. Similarly, researchers have found that human infants have no fear of snakes until about two years of age. Cautionary reactions to snakes begin by age three and a half, and definite fear by the age of four. The fear increases until the age of six, and generally by puberty the intense snake fear is greatly diminished or gone entirely.

Variations in fear of heights studied through the visual cliff experiments described earlier are also found. No clear evidence exists that the human can perceive depth prior to the age of two months. But by the age of two months, when an infant is placed on the deep as opposed to shallow end of the visual cliff experimental apparatus, his heart rate slows, indicating attention. Between six to nine months, however, the infant placed over the deep end will exhibit fear, as judged by increased heart rate.

Infant fear reactions to separation from the mother peak at nine to thirteen months and then wane from thirty months onward. Agoraphobia usually begins at eighteen to thirty-five years of age and in approximately 80 percent of the cases never moves into remission. Fear of animals, a normal feature of childhood, activates between the ages of two and four and then subsides. In terms of general fears, 90 percent of children between the ages of two and fourteen show at least one specific fear. The frequency diminishes with age. The peak occurs at the age of three, and interestingly enough, happens again at age nine to eleven among boys and at eleven for girls. Children's reactions to strangers vary. A stranger elicited fear in 31 percent of two-year-olds, 22 percent of three-year-olds, 7 percent of four-year-olds, and none of the five-year-olds (Jersild and Holmes 1935, 168).

Animal behavior specialist Irenaus Eibl-Eibesfeldt writes in *Human Ethology* (1989), "Some behavior patterns do not have to be fully developed at birth. Some behavior patterns mature during the course of ontogeny. Thus, freshly hatched male ducks show no trace of their species-specific courting patterns. Even if they are raised, however, in complete social isolation, they will nonetheless develop these species-typical courtship behaviors" (19).

The parallel between the above behaviors and their timetable of appearing, peaking, and waning with the development of beliefs that dragons are abroad in the world (not from the beginning of cultural evolution but at a certain "age") is obvious, though not at all clear. The mechanisms that trigger certain innate behaviors to manifest themselves at a particular time in the maturation of the individual are, no doubt, a composite result of the interaction of internal and external factors— between the biochemical and the cultural, as it were. Wallace's previous suggestion of the biochemical aspects of religious conversion, or maze-way resynthesis, seems to suggest that when learned (cultural) responses no longer solve biopsychological problems, the human organism is upset at its deepest physical levels; and this upset leads to a variety of primal releases in the form of hysteria, fear, warfare, and so on. These emotions are brought forward from a brain-space where the dragon lives. It seems possible that the living, breathing dragon results from a concatenation of emotions stimulated into expression as humans experience a shift in their sociocultural existence from the ancient model of the band to the radically different, and not anticipated by the nature of primate history, form of the centralized state, a very nonprimate type of social organization.

It also seems possible that the belief in active dragons correlates with a monotheistic form of religious belief. This is not surprising; most states support religions in which the central god is glossed as analogous to the central leader of the newly formed unicentric polity. The diverse segments of state populations are brought together at a psychospiritual level by the belief in one god in the same way that scattered specializations and social classes are unified under a central leader.

Further, it is tempting to observe that the dragon, as the image of ultimate danger to the life of a complex social group, must logically precede the conception of a good, central god, if the predator hypothesis concerning the nature of the dragon is correct. The "good" to the ancient ancestral primates would have been what is "good" for all primates: safety, food, company of friends, and kinsmen. These conditions are, in fact, normal everyday life for most of the primates, including human beings, most of the time; therefore, there would be no need to single out a conceptual statement of the epitome of good as coming from a single god. Evil, on the other hand, is ultimately about death and cessation of mental, physical, and spiritual life, the purview of the predator. It would seem then that the Great Evil, the dragon, would in evolutionary terms set the stage for an awareness of contrast between itself and a composite entity that is not it, i.e., the good and all-powerful god of the state forms.

Other suggestions regarding the transitional position of the dragon in social-evolutionary terms stem from the targets of the dragon attack, as well as its death by a culture hero. The beast traditionally attacks livestock, crops, and women of childbearing years; that is, it attacks the basis of the future. The culture hero who slays the dragon is also a special protector of maidens, and in ending the life of the dragon, he ends the threat to horticultural and pastoral productivity, thus serving to ensure the future of the population as it moves toward a statelike governmental form.

The relationship between stages of political evolution and belief in the dragon as a real creature also helps explain a common observation made about the Western dragon and the Eastern dragon. In most general accounts of dragon lore, the Eastern dragon (of China, Korea, Japan) is benevolent, friendly, and symbolic of imperial office and authority, whereas the Western dragon is bloodthirsty, antisocial, and violent, the quintessential image of evil. This Eastern dragon, the friendly consort of emperors, is being described from a point in Chinese history far advanced, relative to Western state development, in political centralization and control. It is not that the Eastern dragon is friendly and the Western dragon decidedly unfriendly; it is that the comparative descriptions that support the good-versus-evil comparison were made at two different points in a state's evolutionary trajectory and that China was advanced beyond the West at the time of comparison. If the observation of the Western dragon that forms the typical basis of comparison with the Eastern dragon had been made a few centuries later, the Western dragon would be seen on the shields and coats of arms of heads of Western states, a creature clearly symbolic of earthly power, as in the Chinese case. Similarly, in Africa the kings of the Benin as well as those of the Dahomey were depicted as half human, half dragon in state art.

Though I have used the European historical belief in living dragons to suggest some connection to the shift from earlier multicentric forms to more modern unicentric forms, the model I am suggesting holds for the majority of cases in which the dragon worldwide has been seen to be real. The New World cases of the Inca, Mayan, and Aztec dragons are found in the context of centralized political forms, pre-states, ancient kingdoms, and primitive states. Likewise, the images of winged serpents and *uktenas* found in the archaeological and ethnological record of the American Southeast are connected to forms of social life in which hereditary chieftains held sway over castes of nobles, warriors, and commoners in large urban populations. One found at the site of Cahokia, a Native American town dating between 1050 and 1250 along the confluence of the Missouri and Mississippi Rivers, covered an area of five square miles and supported a population of between 30,000 and 40,000 people. The same can be said for the context of the belief in Pululukon among the Pueblo Indians of the American Southwest. These societies were (are) highly organized urban populations with centralized leadership. The dragons of Hawaii lived during the rise of the kingdom found when the first Europeans entered the islands. The New Guinea dragons co-exist with interior New Guinea groups, such as the Dani, who were moving from scattered village organization to a centralized type of structure based on their chronic warfare and the concomitant rise of the war leader, a standard scenario worldwide during the rise of centralized polities. The same evolutionary correlation between rising centralized forms and the belief in real dragons clearly exists also in China, Japan, Southeast Asia, the Near East, India, and Africa.

FATE OF
THE DRAGONS

ow are peoples of diverse cultures all over the world able to express through their arts the existence of a fantastic, flying, many-toothed, reptilian monster—which never existed? Additionally, how are they able to relate the same fundamental story about the animal's behavior, strengths and weaknesses, nature, breath, facial features, haunts, and proclivities?

Explanations put forth in the past have been unfocused, as if the subject matter of the dragon made modern scholars skittish. It seems that most specialists wish to move directly to the assumption that the dragon has no physical basis in reality; that it is powerful, yes, but after all, a mere symbol and therefore by definition inherently nonexistent and empty. Is this reluctance by contemporary scholars to offer materialistic explanations of the dragon—instead immediately relegating the dragon to symbol, and therefore by definition to an unreal status—a faint echo of the fear of the dragon carried by our kind through the millennia even into the halls of academe?

The puzzle of dragon lore is that, even if the dragon is pure imagination, why does it look the way it looks? Why does a dragon look like a dragon? Some writers have suggested that the dragon might be the result of primordial "memories" in the human line, passed down from the days of the dinosaurs. That idea fails for two reasons. Dinosaurs were extinct more than 60 million years before the first upright-walking, tool-using ancestor of modern humans walked the earth. Second, even though the most ancient ancestral roots of the human line existed at the time of the dinosaur, they would have been but tiny snacks for the large reptiles of the Jurassic period, and probably not systematically preyed upon. Even if they were, our primal ancestors would come to have a relatively longer history with the three basic primate predators of the contemporary era than with the dinosaurs, thus tilting the scale in favor of the three predators and not the dinosaurs as the most likely dragon models.

Some who reject the dinosaur as the source of the dragon suggest that the fossil remains of dinosaurs led to the tales of the world-dragon. The problems with this hypothesis are many. Clearly recognizable dinosaur skeletons are few, and before modern techniques to clear land, dynamite mountainsides for roads, excavate with great earthmoving machines, mine with bit and drill, and tunnel, uncovering dinosaur fossil remains would, of course, have been rare.

Cultures to a great degree provide the stuff with which we think about the world. As I observed in the opening chapter, a fossilized footprint of a giant, three-toed creature from the Jurassic period would have been perceived as the footprint of *piamupits,* the cannibal owl, by the traditional Comanche Indians of the southern Great Plains, and as a giant, fire-breathing lizard by an English peasant of the eleventh century A.D. Finally, even if there were thousands of clearly identifiable complete dinosaur fossils (and there are not), they could not provide an explanation for the widely dispersed common notions concerning the dragon's behavior and specific facial features—horns, crests, beards, piercing eyes, sharp teeth, aggression toward young women, poisonous breath, reptilian body, tendency to live in deep pools or dank caves, and fascination with obtaining and guarding treasure.

Another hypothesis suggests beasts like the Komodo dragon, *Varanus komodoensis,* of Indonesia as the origin of dragon mythology. This and other species of the great monitor lizards are as close to living dragons as can be found. However, the Komodo dragon, discovered by the Western world only in the early twentieth century, has had a very restricted range throughout its long history. It does not seem likely that a rare animal from the Lesser Sunda Islands of Indonesia could have been the model for the universal dragon. It lives far off the beaten path, which, of course, is the reason it still lives. And even if the Komodo dragon were the model, how could all the specifics of the dragon's look and behavior be derived universally from observing a monitor lizard? The same can be said for the python or the "flying dragon" lizard of Java or the alligator and crocodile as the models of the world-dragon.

Finally, most of the literature that attempts to discuss the dragon in some sort of scholarly fashion falls into either mythological studies or symbolic analysis in literature. In both cases, the dragon is interpreted as symbol of this or that but never really identified. Its shape and nature are not explained; the writers who deal with dragon-as-symbol assume that it somehow leapt from human consciousness fully formed, and do not wonder why this thing spawned by the mind should look and act exactly as it does.

The weakest of all arguments simply holds that the dragon springs from the imagination. That, of course, does not explain its universality, appearance, or behavior. Humans are wonderful at imagining, and as far as we know, we may be the only animal in the world with this talent. No human being, however, can imagine what he cannot image, or go beyond what his culture and education give him to imagine. Before the dragon idea existed, no one could recognize the footprint of a dragon. So the problem returns: What is the source of the dragon that can be imagined, and why do we humans recognize it when we see it or hear it described to us?

It was an afternoon's study of some scientific articles concerning the behavior of vervet monkeys in the face of attack by their three basic predators—snake, raptor, and leopard—that triggered the idea that the world-dragon was in some way specifically connected to the predators of arboreal primates. Further study revealed not only that vervets are hunted by the snake, raptor, and tree-climbing carnivore, but also that this is a very typical relationship for arboreal primates in all parts of the world. Specific reactions to alarm calls identifying various types of predators have been demonstrated globally in arboreal primate populations, further evidence that the vervet monkey situation is indicative of a widespread behavior pattern among arboreal primates.

Natural selection theory, focusing on the nature of behavior-gene feedback, presents the idea that extant universal behaviors might be understood as the result of environmental pressures on an ancient population. This selective pressure would favor certain individuals who possess the qualities that assist survival in a given environment and act to eliminate those with less adaptive capabilities. Natural selection serves to ensure that the genetic inheritance of a successful member of a population is sent forward into the next generation, there to be refined by the great process of natural selection even further.

The innate predator responses of arboreal primates can be understood as the result of our ancient primate ancestors' struggle to survive and propagate for millions of years in the midst of three types of killers who sought them for a meal. The innate aspect means that this complex of predator recognition and response must be "hardwired," built into the brain. This being so, the genetic propensity to recognize and react to the presence of the snake, raptor, and big carnivore has come through the generations of our forebears, deeply etched by time and the inherent intensity and absoluteness of confrontation with the killers. We find it in animal phobias and other prey-related phobias, such as fear of open spaces.

Many studies that suggest that the brain operates in terms of chunking, lumping, grouping, indexing, and biogramming help to explain how the arboreal primate reaction merged the three predators into the composite predator, the dragon, at a point in human evolution when the arboreal existence was slowly giving way to terrestrial life. Roughly speaking, this took place 3 to 4 million years ago during the development of the early forms of bipedal, upright, tool making creatures such as *Australopithecus.*

For hundreds of thousands of years the dragon slept, perhaps decaying, perhaps existing as some nightmare in the troubled thoughts of the ancient humans. It was not capable of finding expression until art and language had sufficiently evolved, allowing for increasingly fanciful and ultimately local cultural manifestations, maintaining to this day its shape and nature. Though we glimpse the dragon in the world of the ancient bandsmen, it does not spring into life from the murky depths of the primate brain until a particular point in cultural evolution, specifically that point where a multicentric, or loosely organized, polity moves toward centralization and ultimately statehood.

At this point the dragon is confronted by agents of the new order, the culture hero. Typically in armor and bearing a sword (a scenario even existing among the *uktena* combatants of ancient Cherokee Indian times), he kills the beast or tames it; and its image is added to the symbols of state: the crests of European warlords and ancient monarchs, the coats of a Chinese emperor, the shield of an Aztec king, the flag of Wales.

As if the destruction of the dragon cannot be too thorough for the human spirit, the dragon next appears to metamorphose into a palpably unreal character of fantasy. Today the Chinese dragon dancers, a feature of public celebrations anywhere in the world Chinese populations are found, show us that the dragon is empty, generated by human energy, a thing to play with and store away until next year (fig. 23).

The curious feature of the dragon's demise is that even in fantasy it unifies the human community. Once the unification resulted from the fear of the beast, and now we enjoy our final conquest over it by using its name and image in sports teams, in children's folktales, movie monster manifestations, and the shoddy plaster statues of cute, absolutely nonthreatening and whimsical creatures found in all tourist haunts.

In this study I have been guided by biocultural anthropology, a perspective that suggests that certain universal cultural constructs, e.g., dragons, should— in the absence of evidence demonstrating diffusion from some cultural center—be investigated from the standpoint of their possible biological origins. We are biological entities who have shared descent over the millennia from creatures who were arboreal during most of their existence, shaped by life-and-death struggles acted out in the primordial forests of human beginnings. Slowly honed through natural and, later, no doubt also cultural selection, the ancient primates' sensitivity to the three animals that hunted them came to form the substratum of the dragon, a form that we can all perceive as fundamentally the same from

Figure 23: THE DRAGON DANCE OF CHINA. THE DANCER IN THE LEFT FOREGROUND HOLDS A POLE UPON WHICH RESTS THE MAGIC PEARL, A TREASURE PURSUED BY THE DRAGON.

one culture to another. At the same time the dragon's image was of necessity expressed through the customary artistic conventions of a culture manipulated by the artistic individual, thus providing well-nigh infinite variations on the primal, biologically based design motifs. In the end, we find that our psyches are stalked by a fabulous creature whose outlines, etched by evolution and polished by natural selection, remind us that we are still ancient beings possessed of an instinct for dragons.

THE TREE OF LIFE
AND THE THREE
SACRED REALMS

he ideas, experimental findings, field observations, and basic scientific information marshaled thus far to argue for the biological basis of the world-dragon carry in their wake observations concerning the possible biological basis of two other panglobal myth components: the tree of life and the common cosmological belief in the three realms of existence—the here, the below, and the above. These two themes are implicit in the ancient prehuman behaviors and context relating arboreal creatures with the world of their predators.

THE WORLD TREE

The relationship between the tree of life and the dragon is found in many areas. Donald Mackenzie (1994), for example, notes, "In China and Japan there are references in dragon stories to pine trees being forms assumed by dragons. The connection between the tree and the dragon is emphasized by the explanation that when a pine becomes very old it is covered with scales of bark, and ultimately changes into a dragon. By night 'dragon lanterns' (ignis fatuus) are seen on pine trees in marshy places, and on the masts of ships at sea" (83).

Indian *nagas* were likewise described as not only water deities but also tree spirits; and in Gaelic stories, the holy tree is protected by the "beast," one form of which is the dragon that lives in the sacred well.

The tree of life motif, no matter where it is found or in what artistic context, like the dragon is basically the same entity from culture to culture and generally recognizable across cultural-aesthetic boundaries. It is in its most basic form simply an immense tree that is symbolic of life, safety, and fertility and functions to connect the earth and the sky realms (fig. 24). Among the Norsemen, for example, the great ash Yggdrasil, the World Tree, was believed to join the underworld to the world of men and then move up to the home of the gods. Eagles hovered over the great tree, and snakes fed among its roots, while a squirrel named Ratatoskr ran up and down the trunk, carrying messages between the eagle and a dragon that waited at the base of the tree.

In an ancient Scandinavian poem, *Voluspa,* written sometime before the eleventh century, the "seeress" predicts the final fate of the gods and in doing so makes reference to the World Tree and related notion of three levels, or in this case, levels comprised of numbers divisible by three:

> I remember the giants born at the dawn of time,
>> and those who first gave birth to me.
> I know of nine worlds, nine spheres covered by the tree
>> of the world,
> That tree set up in wisdom which grows down to the bosom
>> of the earth. (Cook 1974, 11)

A Han Chinese tomb rubbing from the Chamber of Offerings by Won Yong and dated to A.D. 168 shows a luxuriant tree of life enveloping the world, connecting animal, bird, and human realms to the heavens. Scythians in central Asia worshiped trees and drew tree of life designs on their scabbards. The Lapps of Finland believe that the World Tree unites the three levels of underworld, earth, and sky.

The shamans of Siberia often depict the tree of life on their clothing. In healing rituals they utilize a small, decorated birch tree, cut with nine notches to represent the nine heavens through which the shaman will spiritually pass. It is placed in a specially prepared tent as a symbol of the tree of life, through which the spirit rises to the world above or descends to the world below.

The tree of life appears on bowls between the thirteenth and tenth century B.C. in ancient Assyria. It dates to A.D. 1350 in the Mayer Fejervary Codex from Mexico. In *Black Elk Speaks,* the Oglala Sioux holy man tells of a profound vision in which the tree of life stood at the center of all life, *Wakantanka,* God.

An Egyptian tomb painting from between the sixteenth and fourteenth centuries B.C. in Thebes depicts the sycamore fig, the Egyptian tree of life, where the Great Earth Mother comes to provide all things for the living and to welcome the deceased into her eternal realm. In the famous Javanese Wayang, or "shadow theater," the *kekayon* tree is the sacred center around and upon which the forces of gods and devils battle. In Tibet the *ta'ogs-shing,* the Assembly Tree of the Gods, has roots that reach from the deepest depths of the primordial waters to the realms of the gods.

The prayer carpets of traditional Muslims often depict the gardens of paradise built around the central motif of the tree of life, with its associated symbols of flight and ascent. An eighth-century illumination from Ireland shows two dragons climbing on the tree of life, and in a painting by Pacino Da Bonaguido, a fourteenth-century Italian artist, we see the life of Christ in a tree of life motif with twelve branches.

In Nara, Japan, a seventh-century altar bas-relief at the Tamamushi temple depicts a tree of life. In Buddhist cultures, because of the centrality of the Bo under which Siddhartha Gautama, the Buddha, experienced *Nirvana,* Enlightenment, the tree of life is a very widespread design theme.

The Or-Danom Dayak of Borneo believe that the tree of life grows from the belly of a giant serpent that lives in the underworld; and for the Navajo Indians of the southwestern United States, the tree of life is a giant, sacred corn plant, rooted in the deepest earth and ascending to the heavens. The Navajo say that the "path of blessing" runs through the cosmic cornstalk, and it symbolizes life, health, and well-being. Their myths tell that their gods often travel through various dimensions in the center of the cornstalk.

Figure 24: THE OLMEC, A COMPLEX CIVILIZATION OF EASTERN MEXICO THAT PREDATES THE AZTEC AND THE MAYA, DEPICTED THE TREE OF LIFE IN THIS FASHION.

The Navajo version of the tree of life points to another aspect of this motif. Sometimes the basic feature of the tree, its vertical trunk, is isolated and shaped like a pole, pillar, stupa, mountain, obelisk, or ladder, to name a few of the most common abstracted or refined images. Sometimes the basic image is distilled even further to represent the Axis Mundi, or center of the world.

A good example of how the tree can literally become a pillar is found in the Egyptian hieroglyph meaning "duration and stability." The pillar is based on a symbol, the Djed Pillar, for the immortal god Osiris. The image is that of a tree with the branches removed, leaving the trunk, or pillar. In spring festivals in ancient rural England where celebrations were based on the reverence for life and fertility, the celebrants danced around a maypole, a custom that has persisted in the United States, usually in rural areas, to the present day.

Poles were central images in the mythology and religious behaviors of many native American peoples. The Chickasaw and Choctaw of Mississippi tell in their origin myths of a sacred pole that led them from distant lands in the west into the fertile Mississippi River Valley. Archaeologists excavating in Georgia and Alabama find evidence of poles, some as large as three feet in diameter, erected in plaza areas around which council houses and homes of the elites were built. Early explorers in the Southeast described these poles as eight to ten feet high and recounted the many ritual activities that took place around them.

Indians of the High Plains, peoples like the Blackfoot, Lakota, Cheyenne, Crow, Arapaho, and Kiowa, practiced as their central tribal ritual the sun dance, a world-renewal ceremony that took place early each summer. The central feature of the ritual structure built for the occasion was a tree, cut and erected for the dance, which was believed to connect the human level to the divine. Upon the sun dance tree were placed offerings, and it was while attached to the tree with thongs piercing the flesh of their chests that brave men danced, pulling away from the tree until their skin tore open, releasing the wood pins to which the thongs were attached. In so doing they believed that their god would speak to them through the tree and that their suffering would alleviate that of their people over the coming year. The Plains Indians correctly suggest that this behavior is similar to the Christian account of the crucifixion, where the

cross of Golgotha is the tree upon which Jesus hung in pain and suffering as a prayer for his people. The incorrectly named "totem poles" of the
many Indian cultures along the Pacific Coast from Oregon to Alaska likewise suggest the essential meaning and structure of the tree of life.

In the belief of the Arunta, a native people living in the middle of
Australia, a sacred pole stood at the center of creation where, after making the world, the god Numbakula ascended to the sky-world, never to
be seen again. Like the Chickasaw and Choctaw of Mississippi, the Australian aborigines tell of sticking a pole in the ground at the end of a day's
march and traveling in the direction in which the pole tilted the next
morning. The pole was connecting their world and the upper world.

The Buddhist stupa and the Japanese temple pagoda are meant as
cosmic axes: as connectors between the here, the below, and the above,
and as emblems that promise eternal life if the beliefs for which they stand
are followed in daily life. And as noted earlier, these structures are generally symbolically or terminologically linked to the sacred Bo tree
under which Siddhartha gained enlightenment and became the Buddha.
A tree, this time the *sal* tree, is connected to the place where Buddha was
born. The notion that the tree of life is the source of gods is also found
in the Greek tale in which the god of vegetation, Adonis, is born from
the trunk of a myrrh tree.

The idea that the tree is nurturing to the soul and body occurs
throughout Africa, where many cultures associate sap-filled trees as manifestations of a "divine mother," or source of life. Similarly, the back of a
Chinese bronze mirror from the Tang dynasty, seventh to ninth century,
pictures the sacred tree and describes its sap as the elixir of immortality,
the ambrosia of the gods.

In Islam, as noted previously, the image of the tree of life stands cen-
trally in the celestial gardens. In the tale "The Night Journey," when
Muhammad traveled into the depths and then ascended from Mecca, the
center of Islam, into the seven planetary spheres that populate the heavens, his journey is sometimes through a tree and sometimes up a ladder.

In Japan trees are often decorated with a *shime-nawa,* a rope of
twisted rice straw from which hang white paper strips cut in a zigzag
design, a symbol suggesting the Shinto idea that the tree houses a *kami,*
or spirit. The famous Druids, priests of the Celts, are widely described in

Roman accounts as worshipers of trees; and in many rural villages in India today, the citizen venerate a tree, usually a large, old, or dramatic one, as sacred and symbolic of birth, death, and rebirth. The Jewish menorah, the seven-branched candleholder, originally was derived from an ancient Mesopotamian tree of life symbol. The Christmas tree and the Washington Monument as modern cultural emblems might be related to the more exotic examples of the tree of life motif found above.

James Frazer, author of the classical anthropological study of religion *The Golden Bough* (1961) was very much interested in the worldwide dispersal of ideas that celebrate trees as sacred. His work adds two related ideas to the tree of life motif: that groves of trees may be considered sacred, and that the tree itself may be the subject of worship. He notes the probability that the Teutonic word for "temple" derives from the ancient German concept that certain small woods were sacred sanctuaries. The Celts, of course, are noted for the oak-grove worshiping of the Druids. Near Uppsala, the old religious capital of Sweden, is a sacred grove. The Slavs, Lithuanians, Greeks, and Italians all have tree worship in their early histories. The seriousness of sacred grove worship among the Germans is suggested by the severity of an old German penalty for one who dared to strip bark from a standing tree. The criminal's navel was cut out and nailed to the tree scar resulting from the stripped bark. Then, according to Frazer, he was driven round and round the tree "till all his guts were wound about its trunk" (41).

In the Forum of ancient Rome, the center of Roman life, the ancient fig tree of Romulus was worshiped. Not far away, on the Palatine Hill, a dogwood tree grew that was considered sacred by the Romans.

Frazer discusses many cultures in which trees are considered both sacred and conscious, a sampling of which follows: the Finnish-Ugrian peoples, the tribes of the Volga, the Ostyaks and Woguls of Siberia, the Dyaks of Borneo, the Fiji Islanders, the ancient Chinese, American Indians of the Upper Missouri River, the Ojibway of Canada, the peasant villagers of Austria, the Dieri of south Australia, the Bontoc of Luzon, the Miao-Kia of western China, the Lkungen Indians of British Columbia, the Siaoo of the East Indians, the Warramunga of central Australia, and the Galla of East Africa.

Like the dragon, the tree of life concept and design is found world-wide, and it, like the dragon, is variously rendered from culture to culture. It is universally recognizable and carries everywhere a complex of ideas that associate the sacred tree (pillar/pole/obelisk/grove) with fertility, life, and birth: the future.

The Tripartite Cosmos

The sacred tree of the Norsemen, Yggdrasil, mentioned at the outset of this chapter, clearly illustrates the second dimension of myth to be addressed, a dimension related to the tree of life and to the basic argument for the origin of the dragon image in world culture. Conveniently for our working hypothesis, Yggdrasil is generally depicted with a dragon at its base. Serpents crawl in its roots, eagles float in the top reaches, and a furry, four-footed animal (in the Norse case, a squirrel) traverses the trunk connecting the above and the below. The connection of the tree of life with three levels is widespread. Alexander Eliot (1976) writes,

> There is a quite remarkable consistency in the use and symbolic significance of the tree in almost all cultures, and in the most ancient myths. Its original mythic function is as the center of the world. The tree itself usually incorporates three levels: its roots grow down through the earth to the underworld, while the trunk rises through the world of men and holds the crown up toward the unattainable heights of heaven. . . . It is the symbol of life. (110)

The here, the below, and the above probably comprise the most fundamental expression of cosmological structure found in the world. And even when the number is not three, the tripartite structure can be maintained when the numbers are divisible by three as in the above cases. For example, there may be a singular here but a three-level pattern to the above and below, as among many tribes of the Southeast cultural area, or a here, above, and below with four directions on the here level (and sometimes on the above and below levels as well) among many Plains Indian cultures. Further, the world's most populated religions all feature a clearly delineated three-level picture of the cosmic world—here, heaven, hell. The below commonly serves as the realm of creatures of the dark, often depicted as reptilian, and the above, the realms of light where flying beings abound. The creatures of the here generally share common features with humans, also creatures of the here, but are definitely affected by the powers of the above and below. The major gods of the world are commonly depicted as descending from the above to the below, as well as ascending from the below to the above, like the dragon who carries the image of the above in its wings, the here in its claws and horns, and the below in its reptilian aspect. The One God is a dragon transformed by the rise of state consciousness religions to be a force of all dimensions that are on the side of the Good, who have the formula (prayers, rituals, priests) to bind the great power of the god/dragon to the control of states.

Examples of a three-level cosmos not only abound in contemporary Asian-rooted religions such as Christianity, Judaism, Hinduism, Islam, and Buddhism but are also found in all parts of the world and in a wide variety of technological contexts, from hunting bands to horticultural village life to modern urban societies. As with the dragon and the tree of life motif, the tripartite cosmos will demonstrate many variations as we move in our survey from culture to culture, but all will have the fundamental concept of some version of the here, the above, and the below.

Reindeer herders of Siberia, peoples such as the Tungus and Yakuts, believe that there are "three worlds." In the lower world reside ancestral spirits, while the middle world is the abode of living humans; and the upper or sky world houses vague sky spirits as well as the powerful spirits of Sun, Moon, and Stars.

The Dyak peoples of Borneo, small-scale farmers and gatherers of Melanesia, picture the cosmos as a house with a tree growing through the middle of it. The branches of the tree, commanded by an eagle, represent the upper world; the floor of the house, this world; and the roots of the trees, among which a dragonlike serpent slithers, the lower world.

The Norsemen held a similar idea in which the upper world, the home of the gods, is watched over by an eagle, and the underworld, dark and inhospitable, is commanded by giant snakes. The world of living humans is the world of the here and now. Also reminiscent of the Dyak peoples, the Norsemen often portrayed a great tree as the emblem of the upper, middle, and lower worlds.

The San, hunters and gatherers of southwest Africa and the Kalahari Desert, believe that the earth was created by the supreme being N!adima, who lives with his wife in the upper reaches of the sky world. Land, the second level of the San cosmos, is the home of the San, while the third level, the underworld, is populated with monsters and spirits of the dead.

In the American Southwest, peoples such as the Zuni, Hopi, Tewa, and Keresans believed in a tripartite cosmos, each level having a variety of sub-levels. Likewise, the Iroquis Indians of the Northeast (a farming, trading, and hunting people to whom the earlier English colonists referred as the Five Nations and who controlled vast territories from south-central New York State to Lake Ontario) saw the cosmos as composed of three tiers. The sky world and the underworld stood as extremes and in opposition to each other. The sky world represented order, goodness, and light, while in the underworld dwelled chaos, evil, darkness, and death. The in-between world was that of everyday human experience. A single pine tree with five white roots symbolized the Iroquois confederation.

Native Americans of the Southeast, peoples such as the Creeks, Choctaw, Chickasaw, and Cherokee, believed this world, the realm of everyday life, to be a circular island that rested upon a primordial sea. The upperworld was peopled by the Sun, Moon, and large perfect specimens, or "Kings," of all the creatures that lived on this world. In the underworld, monstrous entities inhabited a place of darkness and confusion.

The nomadic, bison-hunting Lakota of the northern Great Plains believed that before the creation of the earth, the gods lived in a celestial domain; and the ancestors of humans lived, without culture, in a dark and forbidding underworld. In a series of soap-opera-like events, the chief of the gods, Takuskanskan, became angry when the spider trickster Inktomi seduced Ite, daughter of Old Man and Old Woman, into having an illicit affair with Sun (who was rightfully married to Moon, the mother of his daughter Wohpe, or Falling Star). Takuskanskan created the earth and banished Old Man, Old Woman, Ite, and Wohpe to its surface. Inktomi, out of boredom, acted on a request by Ite to find company for the gods. Inktomi, in the guise of a wolf, traveled into the underworld, located a village of humans, and convinced one of them, Tokahe, to move to the earth's surface. Tokahe, called the First, later brought others to the surface, and these were thought to be the first Lakota.

South of the Lakota, and like them nomadic buffalo hunters, lived the Cheyenne. They believed in Heammawihio, a supreme being of great knowledge who eons ago left the earth to live in the sky. He is the Wise One Above, and his emblem is the sun. The underworld is controlled by Aktunowihio, the Wise One Below, while the earth is seen as a separate entity but related to the topmost layer of the underworld.

The Iroquois Indian confederation—Seneca, Mohawk, Oneida, Onondaga, Cayuga—who in ancient times hunted and farmed throughout much of New York State as well as parts of Canada and Pennsylvania, believed in a tripartite cosmos in which the spirit forces in each ascending level possessed broader power and control than the spirit forces on the layers beneath. The highest level comprised Spirit Forces beyond the Sky and contained the Four Beings, Creator, and Handsome Lake. The second tier, Spirit Forces in the Sky, contained Wind, Thunderers, Sun, Moon, and Stars. The third level, Spirit Forces on Earth, comprised People, Animals, Earth, Grasses, Birds, Fruit, Trees, Water, and the Three Sisters—corn, beans, and squash.

In the Far North, in the frigid lands stretching from the northern territories of Canada to Greenland, live the Inuit (Eskimo). Their cosmology describes Adlivun, "those who live beneath us," and its mistress Sedna. Adlivun is typically depicted at the bottom of the sea. Here, Sedna lives in a house made of reflective walls, where she is guarded by a strange doglike creature with black hindquarters and no tail. She is the central focus of the Inuit in these regions, since they believe that she supplies the fish and animals of the sea. Souls of the dead come to Sedna until they become *adliparmio,* or "at rest," at which time they go to a heaven-like place, which the Inuit see as "below," or a hell-like place, "above." The upper world, associated with Sila, a sky spirit who controls the sun, is cold, with nothing to eat; while the lower world, associated with Sedna, is the reward for those who in life were good workers and hunters, those who accomplished great feats, and those who died by violence or in childbirth.

In Mesoamerica the Maya, city builders to rival the Aztec, thought of the heavens as thirteen layers, each presided over by a principal god. The lowest of the thirteen layers became the earth's surface, stage of human activity, while the underworld had nine layers, the lowest of which, Metnal, was ruled over by Ah Puch, the Lord of Death. A study of a modern Mayan community, the northern Lacandon Maya of south-eastern Chipas, Mexico, revealed another variation of the threefold cosmic classification. The Lacandon Maya believe in a cosmos that has three major levels and two others of little to no importance in daily life. In the underworld reside the souls of the dead, and inhabiting the earth, humans and terrestrial deities. The Celestial God's Sky is the kingdom of sky gods as well as Sun, Moon, and Stars. The two additional layers are "higher" levels. One is called K'akoch's Layer of Sky, where the creator god K'akoch lives but remains separate from the affairs of humans; and the other is the Minor God's Sky, the most remote realm conceivable, where all is cold and dark.

The Aymara of Bolivia display their understanding of the three-leveled cosmos in many ways. During the Feast of the Dead, the Aymara build in their kitchens a *mesa,* or "table" for the dead, which is constructed of three levels. The lowest is covered with samples of coca, apples, bananas, and *chicha*—lowland products—while the the next ascending tier is decorated with cooked potatoes, beer, *oca,* and bread, symbolizing the central lands. A square box forms the third and highest level, where flowers and effigies and products of birds, fish, and cattle are found. The Aymara say that the three-leveled table represents Mount Kaata. Joseph Bastien, author of *Mountain of the Condor* (1978), writes, "The Indians understand the mountain as a solid three-leveled center with an ephemeral heaven above a hollow neatherworld foundation. The Sun, the living and the dead, circulate above, below and around the mountain" (179).

The Yanomamo Indians, a horticultural people with a population of about 20,000 who live in widely scattered villages in Brazil and Venezuela, conceive of the cosmos as four layers. The topmost layer, however, contains nothing that relates to the life of the Yanomamo. Below the top level is the sky world. The Yanomamo believe that people can see only the bottom of the sky world, where the stars, sun, and moon display themselves. They feel, however, that the top of the sky world looks very much like the earth where they live, with jungles and gardens and animals. The Yanomamo believe the souls of the dead go there and carry on an existence into eternity very much like the one they left behind on the earth's surface.

The Yanomamo further believe that the level on which they live was formed when a piece of the sky world broke off and fell down to its present location. The bottom-most layer, which exists underneath the earth, came about when a very heavy piece of the sky world fell onto a particular village with such force that it pushed it through the earth's surface to a new lower level. However, since the catastrophe left their gardens and hunting grounds behind when their village was driven below, the people of that level are thought to be cannibals who are particularly fond of preying on the souls of children.

The same questions can be posed about the three sacred levels and the tree of life that were asked about the dragon: Why? Why does it look the way it does? What is the source of the common images and meanings that attach to such global myth elements as dragons, trees of life, and the three sacred levels? Cultures have attempted various ways to depict the axis of the world, the connecting link from here to there. In some, the image of cosmic connection is a mountain (as with the Aymara just discussed), in some a rainbow upon which gods glide. In others, clouds or lightning bolts or sunbeams play the role. But the presence of the tree of life far surpasses other symbols on the world stage, and it is found even where the above images also exist, suggesting that the tree may be older than the others, the result of evolving creative use of fundamentally and biologically based religious symbolism.

Likewise, why the number three? The widespread notion of three cosmic dimensions, like dragon beliefs, is similar in that neither is based in physical fact but yet occurs in cultural units all over the planet. Why not four or seven, two other popular numbers in the organization of cultural materials?

As noted previously, one can simply elicit the argument for the evolution of the dragon and find in natural selection the reasons that the tree of life and the cosmology of three levels are as widespread as the dragon. The roots of the dragon, the tree, and the three levels are all part of what has to be one of the most crucial elements in understanding how culture evolved, the arboreal experience of our most ancient ancestors. If, as with the attempt to understand the dragon, we look at the world from the perspective of our ancient primate ancestors, the tree of life is not mere symbol; it is the most fundamental truth and reality. Likewise, the three levels: they result from the spatial discrimination and sensitivity forced upon ancient primates by the life-and-death encounter with the predators of the sky, of the tree, and of the ground.

In all studies of monkeys, baboons, orangutans, chimpanzees, and lemurs, their first goal in the face of attack is to seek the safety of trees. To gain the tree is to live. This is fundamental in our origins. Obviously those ancient ancestors who lacked the deep connection to the tree were killed, while those who evolved through millennia of predation an instinct to flee and to climb in the face of attack survived, and their genetic propensities with them, to be carried forward into the future generations. The result today is the widespread use of trees as celebrations of life—a gigantic tree (remember the perspective of the small ancient primates) that reaches from the depths of the earth to the heavens.

The importance of the trunk of the tree as pillar, stupa, or obelisk is understandable in that the major drive of the ancient arboreal ancestors was to access the trunk, not necessarily the branches. The trunk provided the main highway up and down in the run for life—up from the leopard, down from the eagle, and up and down, depending on the location of the hunting arboreal snake.

The realities of primate evolution, which include the role of predators as mechanisms of natural selection, have biologically predisposed humans to a sensitivity to the dragon image, as well as to the tree of life motif and the tripartite cosmos. The near-universal presence of these mythic entities and conditions cannot be explained by appeal to diffusion from a single source. Further, the unique complexity of the dragon, tree of life, and tripartite cosmos forestalls any attempt to explain their universal presence by an appeal to independent invention. A biocultural mode of explanation seems to account for the mythic universals under discussion more elegantly than alternative theories.

MORE TALES
OF THE GREAT WORM

ragons! Dragons! Dragons! They are everywhere. They ramble through space and time as no other beast, imaginary or real, has ever done. Look into world mythology; they are there. Peek into the most remote corners of the world, and you will find them. Walk down the main street of any modern city, scan the store windows, and I guarantee you will eventually see one.

Professional hockey claims the San Antonio Dragons; the American Arena Football League, the Portland Forest Dragons; and the National Football League's European division, the Barcelona Dragons. The Des Moines Dragons compete in the International Basketball Association, while the Orlando Dragons play in an all-women's baseball league. The Bethesda Dragons won the Under-Eleven Maryland State Soccer Championship in 1996. The Battle Dragons fight it out in the Paintball competition in Michigan, and the Sonoma Sea Dragons win tournaments in the California swim club competition. In Australia, the St. George Dragons play other members of the Australian National Rugby League, while in Brisbane, the Dragon Vollyball Association maintains offices and an extensive website for its fans. In the United Kingdom, the Durham

City Dragons play in the U.K. Ice Hockey League, and the U.K. rugby world includes the Doncaster Dragons.

In the People's Republic of the Congo, hundreds of native peoples as well as foreign visitors have reported seeing a creature called the *mokele-mbembe*. They describe a large dinosaurlike body and four massive legs with clawed feet, a thick, tapering tail, and a long, slender neck. About the size of an elephant, it reaches a total length of thirty feet. It is said to live in the trackless wastes of the Likouala swamps in the Congo. Reports of its existence have been so persuasive in modern times that in the 1980s a number of expeditions, including one mounted by biologist Roy Mackal of the University of Chicago, went in search of it.

What drew Professor Mackal into the field was obviously not the search for a dragon but the interesting fact that all of the many eyewitness accounts of the *mokele-mbembe* seemed to be describing a small sauropod dinosaur; and of course, it is well known that dinosaurs have been extinct for many millions of years and were never seen by humans. Still, the natives living on the edge of the Likouala swamp were shown pictures of nonlocal animals as well as prehistoric animals, and every time they identified the sauropod dinosaur as *mokele-mbembe*.

The Greek myth dealing with the battle between Zeus and the dragon called Typhon, a tale alluded to in the text, has a few other exciting plot elements that were not detailed earlier. Zeus and the other gods ran from Typhon and took refuge in Egypt; but after being accused of cowardice, Zeus returned to give battle to Typhon. Zeus lost the first few encounters with the creature that could hurl entire mountains but finally wounded him in a battle in Thrace and chased him to Sicily, where he succeeded in crushing the beast under Mount Aetna.

Gaea, an ancient Greek earth goddess impregnated by a single drop of blood that fell from Typhon's head, gave birth to the autochthons Actaeus, the first king of Athens; Cecrops, the second king of Athens; and Crannaus, successor to Cecrops, who renamed his kingdom Attica after his daughter Atthis. Legend describes Actaeus, Cecrops, and Crannaus with human heads and large reptilian bodies featuring four clawed feet and stunted wings.

The Greek tale of Zagreus, son of Demeter the Earth Mother, features his resurrection, after his dismemberment at the hands of the

Titans, as a horned serpent. In the ceremonies of Dionysus-Sabazius, a snake was passed over the body of the initiate as the assembled dignitaries chanted, "The Bull is the father of the Dragon, and the Dragon is the father of the Bull." Another related Greek dragon reference states, "A serpent never becomes a flying dragon until it has devoured another serpent" (Charbonneau-Lassay 1991, 154–55).

Just as the Greeks believed that both monsters and heroes were spawned by the gods, so too did the monstrous Typhon beget, with the serpent-bodied Echidna, the chimera and the hydra Ladon, protector of the garden of Hesperides and its golden apples. The chimera was described in a number of ways. Fundamentally it was a fire-breathing creature with a body that was, from front to back, that of a lion, a goat, and a dragon. Sometimes it was depicted as lion-headed, with a living serpent for a tail. Homer, in Book VI of the *Iliad,* showed the chimera as capable of breathing fire. The *Aeneid* stated that the creature was native to Lycia.

The most famous Greek hydra dragon, Ladon, the Lernaean hydra, was killed by Hercules as the second of his legendary twelve labors at the order of Eurystheus, king of Mycenae. Ladon, born in the swamp of Lerna in southern Greece, destroyed farms, villages, and livestock, turning the district of Argolis into a sterile wasteland. Hercules confronted Ladon at its lair, a dank cavern near Amymone, and though Hercules had help in the battle from his companion Iolaus, so did the hydra. A huge crab snapped at Hercules' feet as he struggled with the dragon.

The Greek god Apollo was forced to contend with a potent dragon in the form of Python. The *Homeric Hymn to Apollo* tells of his search for a site on which to build an oracular shrine. After a number of false starts, he arrived at Delphi and began to lay the foundations of his temple. However, he was soon challenged by a female dragon named Delphyne, a savage beast that dwelt in a spring and ravaged the flocks and villages of the people who lived in the area. In later versions, the dragon had become a male and was called Python.

The Greek hero Jason, in his quest for the Golden Fleece, confronted a guardian dragon in the service of the king of Colchis. With the help of Medea, he drugged the beast and escaped with the Fleece. Centuries later Alexander the Great, striking out with his armies from Macedonia, reportedly encountered a gigantic, hissing, cave-dwelling dragon so terrifying that his army offered it gifts and worship lest it destroy them.

In later times, the Roman writer Propertius told of a town twenty miles from Rome that was protected by an ancient dragon. The large reptilian creature lived in a deep muddy pit and demanded a novel form of payment for its protection: a pure young maiden with a basket of food lowered into its cave to serve him with her own hands. If she flinched as the dragon sucked the food from her fingers or if she proved impure in heart and body, the dragon would shred her. If her courage and virtue satisfied him, she would be returned to the surface unharmed. The difficult relationship between dragons and maidens repeatedly appears as a theme in worldwide dragon lore.

The Roman army often featured dragon emblems on shields and banners, and a windsock type of military standard was made in the shape of a dragon. The dragon image, perhaps borrowed from the Romans, was also used as a battle standard by the early British kings. Joe Nigg (1995) writes, "The heraldic dragon has the toothed jaw and scaly stomach of a crocodile, pointed ears, the talons of an eagle, the ribbed wings of a bat, and a serpentine tail" (109).

During the First Punic War (264–241 B.C.), when Rome was battling the African city of Carthage over control of Sicily, the Roman army under General Marcus Atilius Regulus confronted a giant serpent during its march on Carthage. As the Roman battalions approached the banks of the Bagrada River, they were met by a snakelike monster one hundred feet in length. Its eyes burned liked fire, and its roar stunned the army's front lines, forcing them to fall back. It lifted its huge body from the reeds along the river and defied the Romans to pass. General Regulus consulted with his captains, and though their troops were armed with many kinds of weapons, covered in armor, and in possession of a number of wall-shattering war machines, they counseled the general not to engage the monster. Regulus wisely backed his forces away from the creature and marched to another point on the river to cross into Carthage.

In many parts of the world, the dragon image is basically that of an unnaturally large snake. However, as a house cat is not a lion, a snake is not a dragon. The sheer mass difference renders the lion a fundamentally different force than a house cat. Likewise, a mere snake does not equate with the hundred-foot-long serpent reportedly confronted by the Romans outside Carthage.

The dragon boats of the Vikings were believed to give these Norse warriors cunning, courage, and keen eyesight. The Vikings drew their dragon images from legends that reached back to the times recorded in the *Aesire,* the sagas of the warrior gods of the Norsemen. It is there that Jormungander, the Midgard Serpent, appears. Son of Loki and Angerboda, the god of evil, this immense serpent sported a dragon's head. When it was brought before Odin the All Wise, he recognized its potential danger and threw it into the depths of the sea. There it was ordered to remain, tail in mouth, girdling the world like the Greek Oroboros until Ragnarok, the Day of the Last Battle, at which time the giants, monsters, and warrior gods would engage in their final struggles, the outcomes of which would define eternity. Thor, the mighty god of thunder, however, was to encounter Jormungander several times, and in the last encounter he was to die.

His first meeting with the great dragon occurred on a fishing trip with his friend the giant Hymir. Thor, his hook baited with an ox head, soon found himself embroiled with the Midgard Serpent. However, just as Thor readied to kill the creature with his famed hammer, Hymir lost his courage and cut Thor's line, releasing the dragon back into the sea. A picture from an Icelandic manuscript dating to 1680 depicts Jormungander about to take Thor's bait. The horned head of the heavy-bodied reptilian beast is about ten times the size of the ox-head bait, and the mouth full of long, sharp teeth. Jormungander's tail is drawn to suggest feathers rather than a reptilian tip, and the creature has two short clawed feet at the forward part of its body.

Eons later, on the Day of the Last Battle, Jormungander rose from the sea to seek combat with Thor, the only warrior god worthy of him. The fight was, of course, incredible. Thor hurled thunderbolts, and Jormungander slashed, roared with mind-rending blasts, writhed, and thundered until Thor finally succeeded in striking him on the head with his great hammer Miolnir. The dreaded Midgard Serpent fell to the ground dead, but minutes later, so too did Thor, killed by the monster's poisonous final breath.

Another Scandinavian dragon, Nidhogg (also Nidhoggr, Nydhogg, Niddhogg), dwelt in the pit called Hvergelmer at the base of Yggdrasil, the World Tree. This place was both a pillar which separated the earth and sky and supported the universe, and the location where the gods rendered judgment. The "Dread Biter," as this dragon was called, chewed nightly at Yggdrasil's roots to destroy the universe, while workmen returned each day to repair the damage. This, according to the Norsemen, would continue forever. Nidhogg, whose main preoccupations were evil and destruction, is rendered in many paintings and drawings as a large lizardlike beast with wings and huge claws and teeth.

Fafnir is perhaps the most well known of the dragons of Norse mythology, due to Wagner's opera *Der Ring des Nibelungen,* which tells of the adventures of the hero Siegfried. The story was also alluded to in *Beowulf, Njal's Saga,* and the thirteenth-century Icelandic *Saga of the Volsungs.* The original legend told of a man named Kriedman who had three sons, Otter, Regin, and Fafnir. When the god Loki accidentally killed Otter, he paid for his actions by offering a great payment in treasure to the father. Fafnir, in time, lusted for his father's gold and finally killed him to possess it. Then, to more effectively guard the treasure, he used his talents as a shape-shifter to transform into a fearsome dragon. To feed himself, he ravaged the villages and farms of the countryside.

Regin, his brother, convinced the knight Sigurd (also known as Siegfried) Volsung that he could gain fame and fortune by killing Fafnir, and together they searched out Fafnir's lair. Knowing that only a sword thrust through the dragon's belly could kill him, Regin and Sigurd dug a pit across the path to the dragon's daily watering hole; and after Sigurd crawled into the hole, Regin covered it with brush. When Fafnir walked over the pit, Sigurd rammed his sword home, killing the dragon. In the myth Fafnir appeared as a large reptilian creature with stunted wings, great teeth and claws, and a breath of fire and smoke. Fafnir was celebrated in many artworks. In the eleventh century a Swedish woman named Sigrid commissioned a large stone carving on an outcropping near a bridge that she had built and dedicated to the memory of her husband, Holmgr. There Fafnir was rendered as a serpentine two-headed dragon.

He appeared again, battling with Sigurd, in carved wooden panels that originally bracketed a medieval church in Norway. The panels show

Sigurd driving his sword into the dragon's stomach. Fafnir appears with gaping mouth, tigerlike head and teeth, and a long reptilian body The original work, the Sigurd Portal, has been moved in recent times to the Oldsaksamlingen of the University of Oslo.

An Old English tale featuring the dragon is the eighth-century heroic saga of the Danish king Beowulf. The poem comprised three basic tales, the third of which told of Beowulf's combat with a dragon who became angered when one of Beowulf's servants discovered his treasure trove and stole a golden cup. The angry dragon vented its rage by rampaging through Beowulf's country, burning villages and killing people and livestock. The hero engaged the beast at the mouth of the dragon's cave as the large winged saurian creature belched flames and poisonous gas. Beowulf was almost devoured when he broke his sword against the dragon's scaly back, but fortunately his companion Wiglaf rushed to his rescue, and together they killed the beast.

Dragon images have fascinated the peoples of the British Isles for centuries. Beowulf carried a shield with a dragon painted on it, as did King Arthur. In time it became the customary battle standard of many English kings. The chiefs of the Celtic knights were called Pendragon, and when such a leader was downed in battle, the event was referred to as "killing a dragon." A dragon decorated Oliver Cromwell's coat of arms, and the creature became a feature of the shields of Henry VII, Henry VIII, and Edward VI. In modern times a red dragon was incorporated into the heraldic ensign of the Prince of Wales, and the same dragon appears on the modern Welsh flag.

A Welsh tale with a curious twist told of the killing of a dragon that terrorized the town of Denbigh, attacking people and flocks from a ruined castle it occupied. The townsmen sought the aid of Sion Bodiau (Sir John of the Thumbs) because he had two thumbs on each hand. Sion tempted the fire-breathing saurian out of its castle, and while it stared in fascination at Sion's strange hands, the knight cut the dragon's head off. Though the town is called Denbigh in English, it is Dim-Bych in Welsh, a phrase that means "No more dragon."

As late as the middle 1800s, the people who lived in the vicinity of Penllyne Castle in Glamorgan, Wales, reported winged serpents (fig. 25). They were also seen at Penmark Place, and snakes with feathered

Figure 25: THIS IMAGE OF A WINGED SERPENT FIRST APPEARED IN THE *HISTORIE OF SERPENTS,* WRITTEN BY EDWARD TOPSELL IN 1608.

wings were described in the Vale of Edeyrnion in 1812. The locals who claimed to have seen them in the early days said they were brightly colored and very beautiful, but because they preyed on the farmers' poultry, they were hunted to extinction.

Many types of dragons were found in the British Isles. Very similar to the winged serpents described above are the *amphipteres*—large, winged, legless serpents with dragon heads. The citizens of Henham in Essex, England, experienced one on May 27 and 28, 1669. Sporting stunted wings, it stood nine feet long, was covered in scales, and had a mouth full of long fangs and two tongues. The villagers succeeded in driving it away by throwing stones at it.

Wyverns were dragons with scales, large batlike wings, and a single pair of legs. Leonardo da Vinci drew a wyvern attacking a lion and clearly expressed its scales, claws, crest, gaping mouth, and wings.

Legless and wingless dragons called worms (also wyrms or wurms) were also found in the British Isles. Specialists in dragon lore consider them to be very ancient dragons, with the Lambton Worm being one of the best known. The story of this dragon revolved around the exploits of John Lambton, heir to Lambton Hall, who one Sunday morning chose to go fishing in the Wear River instead of attending church. He caught a three-foot-long eel-like creature with a large mouth full of sharp teeth and spiked crests running along the top of its dragon head. Considering the thing too ugly to eat, he tossed it into a deep old well.

As the years passed and John left for war, the worm grew to enormous proportions, abandoned the well, and attacked the villagers who lived around Lambton Hall. When John returned from his adventures, he was told by a local witch that he must kill the dragon and afterward the next living being he encountered. The worm proved no problem to the brave knight, but he next saw his father, who had come out to congratulate him on his victory against the creature. John refused to kill his father, and a curse was placed on the Lambton family. For the succeeding nine generations, all Lambton heirs were doomed to die outside their own country.

Witch's curses played a part in the tale of the Laidly Worm. The daughter of a king of Northumbria was cursed and turned into a worm. In the manner of *Sleeping Beauty* with a little of *Beauty and the Beast* thrown in, the prince was required to kiss the hideous worm three times before the beautiful princess Margaret was restored to her human form.

A conventional saurian fire-breathing dragon living in Wantley Lodge in a Yorkshire village was killed by the heir of More Hall during the time of Queen Elizabeth I. He utilized a technique that would appear in a number of dragon-slayer tales found in Greece, France, and Ireland, as well as in the American Indian tale of the dragon-monster Mashenomak. Sir More ordered a special suit of armor covered with spikes to be made at Sheffield. This suit prevented the dragon from swallowing him while he concentrated on defeating the beast, in this case by kicking it stoutly in the rear end. Another fire-breather was killed by Sir John Smith of Deerhurst, England, during the Middle Ages. Sir John placed a huge bowl of milk, of which this dragon was deeply fond, on a trail near the dragon's cave. After the dragon had drunk his fill, he lay down to rest, and Sir John slipped his sword between the otherwise impenetrable scales.

Early French history also resounded with the roar of the dragon. The *guivre* was a reptilian, horned monster whose breath was so toxic that when it touched humans, disease and plague followed. Most dragons, however, had some type of weakness that a potential slayer must discover. In the case of the *guivre,* its flaw was revealed one day by a farmer who removed his clothes to bathe in a stream after a hard morning's work. As he approached the stream, which unbeknownst to him was the home of the local *guivre,* it reared up from the water's edge but quickly turned away when it saw that the farmer was naked. In fact, it even blushed. The inability to face the unclothed human body proved to be its downfall.

The river Huisne in France provided a home to a dragon called the Peluda, who in medieval times lived in the vicinity of the village of La Ferte-Bernard. It was a fire-breather with four stubby legs and turtlelike claws. Its novel body featured a combination of scales along the tail, shaggy green fur, and a mass of needle-sharp quills on its back. When it gamboled in the river Huisne, its enormous size caused flooding that destroyed farms for miles around. It developed a taste for teenage girls; and a young local man, whose fiancé was eaten before his eyes, sought the advice of a wise woman concerning methods to defeat the Peluda. She divulged the monster's weakness, the serpentine tail; and the young man, armed with that knowledge as well as armor and a sharp sword, confronted the beast and killed it. It was said that the Peluda had refused to enter Noah's ark and yet somehow survived the world flood.

A fourteenth-century French tale, *Voeux du Paon,* tells of the count of Anjou and his quest for a bride. After searching for a number of years, he returned to his palace with a beautiful woman named Melusine. Charming and aristocratic, she produced four heirs for the count, but a peculiar habit finally forced the curious count to challenge her. Melusine, the few times that she did attend mass, always left before the priest raised the consecrated chalice before the congregation. One Sunday when she was in attendance, the count placed four knights at the church door. As was her custom, she rose to leave midway through the service but found the door blocked. In a rage, she sent forth a shattering roar, metamorphosed into a dragon, and grabbing two of her children, flew from the church. Her remaining children were to become the foundation for the house of Plantagenet, one of the most prominent royal families of Europe. An eighteenth-century Russian print of Melusine pictures her with a woman's head and a dragon's body. Her serpentine tail has a dragon's head at its tip, and her four feet are likewise rendered as dragon heads.

The dragons of France played a part in early Christian tales, in which they represented Satan or pagan religions, and European saints often killed them. In the sixth century, for example, an enormous winged dragon decided to occupy a cave near a convent located in Poitiers, France. When it began eating the local nuns, the abbess Saint Radegund confronted and killed it by making the sign of the cross. The original *gargouille* described earlier was eventually defeated by Saint Romain, archbishop of Rouen.

Saint Martha faced the terrible Tarasque that hunted along the river Rhone between Avignon and Arles in the Middle Ages. When the Tarasque focused on the village of Nerluc and commenced to methodically destroy everyone and everything in the community, the saint took action. The Tarasque stood somewhat larger than an ox, and its six thick limbs were each equipped with bear paws. Its tail was that of a large serpent with a pointed tip. A horny shell protected its back, and its long teeth were like daggers. Saint Martha, "her holiness, her shield," captured the

Tarasque and led it back to the village by a tether she fashioned from her fragile shawl. The locals promptly killed it.

Saint Columba defeated a Scottish dragon of the Ness River as a demonstration to the local Picts of the superiority of Christianity. The monster later moved into Loch Ness. A brief listing of other saints responsible for defeating various kinds of Western dragons includes Saint Andrew of Aix-en-Provence, Saint Victor of Marseille, Saint George of England, Saint Michael the Archangel, and Saint Armentaire of Draguignan.

The Polish capital city of Krakow was established on a site overlooking the village of Wavel, where the hero Krak killed a huge, purple-winged dragon. To the south in modern times, the people of the Swiss, Austrian, and Bavarian Alps have reported seeing the *Tatzelwurm* (sometimes called the *Stollenwurm* or "clawed worm"), a reptilian creature four to five feet in length with two clawed forelegs and the head of a large cat. In 1921 near Hochfilzen, Austria, such a creature was shot at by a herdsman. A similar creature was seen attacking a herd of pigs near Palermo, Sicily, in 1954. The *Tatzelwurm* is referred to as a drake and is defined as a dragon with a large, scaled serpentine body, sharp slashing teeth, and four heavily clawed feet, but no wings. Fire drakes are said to be capable of shooting fire from their mouths.

In England between the twelfth and sixteenth centuries, "grypeseye," or griffin eggs, were highly prized collectibles, listed in the inventories of noble houses and often made into cups in which beverages thought to possess powerful health-giving qualities were brewed. A putative griffin's paw, taken by a knight in battle, once hung on the wall of Sainte-Chapelle in Paris (Dooling 1991, 404).

Dragons, like all human constructs marked by cultural or learned influences, evolve through time. That the dragons responded to changing social, cultural, and historical environments is amply demonstrated in the shifting history of the dragon called the basilisk, or "little king," by the Greeks and *regulus* by the Romans. Though the cultural rendering of the basilisk (size, superficial physical characteristics, coloring, and shape) will be seen to change through time, its essential dragon nature does not.

Pliny the Elder, in his *Natural History,* presented the basilisk as a type of snake that moved along the ground holding its front half in the air. He described this dragon as about twelve inches in length with a number of bright white marks on its head, a trait that he thought looked like a diadem, or jeweled crown. Later Christian cultures would see it as a cross. The hiss of the basilisk drove other serpents away in fear, and its breath scorched grass and bushes and exploded rocks. Its lethality caused animals that gazed upon it to perish. It could knock birds out of the air with its venomous saliva, and dragon slayers could kill it by holding a mirror so that it looked upon its own deadly visage. The following is a modern account of a dragon sighting:

> On July 30, 1915, during World War I, a German submarine, the U-28, torpedoed the British steamer Iberian near the Fastnet Rock, off Ireland; but less than a minuter after the ship had sunk, a huge underwater explosion blasted a gigantic, writhing monster out of the sea. According to the account later given by the captain of the U-28, it was about 60 feet long and shaped like a crocodile, with a long pointed tail and four limbs with powerful webbed feet. It fell back into the sea a few moments later and disappeared without a trace. (Shuker 1995, 115)

Sightings of sea dragons by sailors have a long history. For example, Captain George Drevar, master of the *Pauline,* made the following entry in the ship's log on January 8, 1875 (fig. 26):

> BARQUE *PAULINE.* JANUARY 8TH, 1875, LAT. 5 13', LONG. 35 W, CAPE ROQUE, NORTH-EAST CORNER OF BRAZIL DISTANT TWENTY MILES, AT 11 A.M.

> The weather is fine and clear, the wind and sea moderate. Observed some black spots on the water, and a whitish pillar, about thirty-five feet high, above them . . . good glasses showed me it was a monster sea-serpent coiled twice around a large sperm whale. The head and tail parts, each about thirty feet long, were acting as levers, twisting itself and victim around with great velocity. They sank out of sight about every two minutes coming to the surface still revolving . . . . the sea in this vicinity like a boiling cauldron . . . a loud and confused noise was distinctly heard. This strange occurence lasted some fifteen minutes. . . . Allowing for two coils around the whale, I think the serpent was about one hundred and sixty or one hundred and seventy feet long and seven or eight

FIGURE 26: ON JANUARY 8, 1875, THE CREW OF THE BARQUE *PAULINE* OBSERVED A SEA SERPENT ATTACKING A WHALE OFF THE COAST OF BRAZIL.

in girth. It was in colour much like a conger ell, and the head, from the mouth being always open, appeared the largest part of the body. . . . I wrote thus little thinking I would ever see the same or a similar monster; but at 7 A.M., July 13th, in the same latitude, and some eighty miles east of San Roque, I was astonished to see the same or a similar monster. It was throwing its head and about forty feet of its body in a horizontal position out of the water as it passed onwards by the stern of our vessel. . . . This statement is strictly true, and the occurrence was witnessed by my officers, half the crew, and myself; and we are ready at any time to testify on oath that it is so, and that we are not in the least mistaken. (Gould 1886, 312–14)

A year later in Asian waters John W. Webster, commander of the *S. S. Nestor,* made this log entry (fig. 27):

Being on the bridge at the time (about 10 A.M.) with the first and third officers, we were surprised by the appearance of an extraordinary monster going in our course and at an equal speed with the vessel, at a distance from us of about six hundred feet. It had a square head and a dragon black and white striped tail, and an immense body, which was quite fifty feet broad when the monster raised it. The head was about twelve feet broad, and appeared to be occasionally, at the extreme, about six feet above the water. When the head was placed on a level with the water, the body was extended to its utmost limit to all appearance, and then the body rose out of the water about two feet, and seemed quite fifty feet broad at those times. The long dragon tail with black and white scales afterwards rose in an undulating motion, in which at one time the head, at another the body, and eventualy the tail, form each in its turn a prominent object above the water. The animal, or whatever it may be called, appeared careless of our proximity, and went our course for about six minutes on our starboard side, and then finally worked around to port side, and remained in view, to the delight of all aboard, for about half an hour. Its length was reckoned to be over two hundred feet. (Gould 1986, 308–9)

Turning to the dragons of Asia (figs. 28, 29, 30), we must acknowledge once more that artistic style will vary from culture to culture, sometimes radically and sometimes, admittedly, only slightly. The drag-

Figure 27: A CRESTED SEA SERPENT ATTACKING A SAILING VESSEL.

Figure 28: CHINESE FIVE-TOED IMPERIAL DRAGONS CAVORT IN THIS STONE PAINTING. THOUGH LACKING WINGS, THE CLOUD MOTIFS INDICATE THAT THE DRAGONS WERE IN FLIGHT.

Figure 29: THIS CHINESE DRAGON DEPICTS THE EARTH, WATER, AND SKY DOMAINS OF THE DRAGON.

FIGURE 30: THE CHINESE DRAGON FLIES OVER THE WAVES IN THE DRAGON GATE IMAGE. NOT SHOWN IN THIS IMAGE, A CARP HAS LEAPT TOWARD THE GATE AND COMES OUT THE OTHER SIDE AS A DRAGON. IT IS AN IMAGE SUGGESTING ATTAINMENT AND GROWTH.

ons of the East, however, are clearly identifiable as dragons by the Western viewer because the dragon is easily recognized everywhere. Also, the ancient and modern arts of the Orient have been familiar to Westerners for many centuries. Asian drawings, paintings, sculpture, and ceramics, which often depict dragons, have been considered desirable as household decorations, particularly by the educated and wealthy of the West, for many years. Dozens of motion pictures and a number of television series have familiarized westerners with the dragon images of China, Korea, and Japan through costumes, painted backdrops, screens and decorations in a variety of mediums utilized for authenticating an "Oriental scene."

An expert minority, however, heatedly contests the comparison of the Western and Eastern dragon. L. Newton Hayes (1922), for example, writes, "We do not know who first attached the English name 'dragon' to the Chinese conception *lung,* but it is hardly fair to the oriental ruler of the sea to be branded with the stigma which accompanies the English designation. . . . A misconception of the use of the word 'dragon' has caused the (devout Western) speakers to confuse the evil monster mentioned in the book of Revelation with the animal so highly revered by the Chinese" (24–25).

Generally, the comments of writers like Hayes are couched in modern Christian associations of the Western dragon as a symbol of Satan. It is not the image of the dragon that these writers dispute, but rather the meaning of the dragon to the East and West. It is not as simple as they would have it, since the dragon's meaning changes over time. In fact, most accounts of Western dragons do not associate the creature with the Christian archnemesis, Satan. Likewise, not all Eastern dragons are benevolent. Those who wish to separate the claimed positive image of the Eastern dragon from the largely negative image of the Western dragon often point to the Eastern dragon's role in generating fecundity, clouds, and rain. However, to such farmers and fishermen, what would be the greatest curse? Too much or too little rain, flooded rivers, or ocean storms: all the purview of the *lungs,* or dragons. In fact, the worst floods were generally ascribed to a dragon's reaction to some sort of untoward mortal behavior.

The sea-dragon kings were believed to live in opulent underwater palaces, where they fed on pearls. When they moved their four-mile-long scaly bodies, earthquakes resulted. Their muzzles were whiskered, and from their gaping mouths came such a fiery breath that, even underwater, whole schools of fish would be roasted. The ancient Chinese believed that when sea dragons rose to the surface, they generated typhoons, the great storms that ripped houses apart, destroyed crops, and flooded the countryside.

During the Han period, Chinese emperors utilized the dragon as their central emblem, as did many of the early kings in Europe. The emperor's throne was "the dragon's seat"; his clothing, "the dragon's robe"; his face, "the dragon's face"; and when he died, he was believed to ride into the heavens on the back of a dragon.

Lu Tian (A.D. 1042–1102) identified a number of dragon types in the *Bei Ya*. He wrote that if the dragon had scales, it was called *jiao long;* but if it had wings, it was designated *ying long.* A dragon with horns was *qiu long,* and one without horns was *chi long.*

Another popular breakdown of Chinese dragon types includes *Tien-lung,* the Celestial Dragon who guards the palaces of the gods; *Shen-lung,* the controller of wind and rain; *Ti-lung,* the Earth Dragon, who is in charge of rivers and all bodies of water; and *Fut's-lung,* the Underworld Dragon, who guards treasures, metals, and precious stones. In addition, the rivers of China are each under the control of separate dragons, who in turn are all controlled by *Chien-tang,* a three-hundred-yard-long scarlet beast with a flaming red mane. Eastern dragons often have horns, beards, tufts of hair, and sometimes feathers at either shoulder. They are occasionally shown with a few long whiskers, also referred to as "feelers," growing from their large-mouthed muzzles.

Some Eastern dragons are thought to have possessed a magical pearl, located in the head or mouth or under the chin, that was capable of granting wishes. It could bring clouds and rain by breathing in a special way, and its flight created thunder and lightning. The Chinese dragon is often described with spines or crests emanating from its back.

Now to some specific visual representations of the Chinese dragon. The first examples are from Abe Capek's fascinating book *Chinese Stone-Pictures* (1962). The pictures represent a cateogry of art called *t'a-pen*—in English, "stone rubbings." Figures 31, 32, 33, and 34 show rubbings of decorative carvings found at a Han period tomb built around A.D. 100.

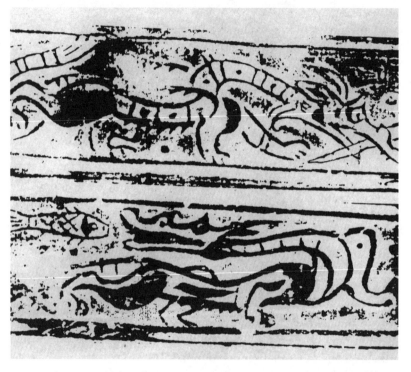

FIGURE 31: ONE OF THE MANY VERSIONS OF CHINESE DRAGONS.
NOTE THE CLOSE RELATIONSHIP BETWEEN THE SHAPE OF THE CHINESE
DRAGON AND THE DRAGONS OF THE INUIT AND OTHERS.

Figure 32: A CHINESE DRAGON WITH SPOTS, HORNS, TALONS, AND WINGS FIGHTS A CULTURAL HERO, GENERALLY DEPICTED IN THE TALE OF THE WORLD-DRAGON AS WIELDING A SWORD.

Figure 33: THIS DRAGON DATES TO 206 B.C. AND WAS FOUND AT THE INAN SITE IN CHINA. THE SCALES, WINGS, LARGE TEETH, HORNS, AND TALONS OF THE WORLD-DRAGON ARE CLEARLY INDICATED.

FIGURE 34: ANOTHER DRAGON IMAGE FROM THE INAN SITE IN CHINA. THIS IMAGE IS CALLED "THE DRAGON SHOW."

The dragon is a four-footed, clawed saurian with horns, serpentine tail, and vestiges of spiky crests down his neck. In several of the renderings, a snakelike tongue protrudes from its mouth. Its relationship to water is indicated in figure 31, where a fish swims before the dragon's mouth. There is also an Oroboros-type theme here in that each dragon is biting the tail of the dragon in front of it.

Rubbings from the tomb of Wu Liang Tz'u portray a variety of dragon images as well as dragon costumes. In figure 32 a typical dragon slayer, sword and shield in hand, attacks a dragon that fundamentally looks like the images described above, in that it has a snakelike body, massive claws, horns, a large mouth, and a protruding tongue. However, in this case, stylized, perhaps winglike, protrusions twine from its shoulders as well as from its lower back.

Another rubbing from the Wu Liang Tz'u tomb (fig. 33), entitled *The Dragon Show* by Capek, shows a creature that stylistically differs again from the above-mentioned images, but retains the fundamental dragon look with its scaled body, four clawed feet, horns, catlike face with gaping mouth, sharp teeth, and abbreviated wings clearly rendered at the shoulder. Figure 34, also from the Wu Liang Tz'u tomb, shows a circus wagon with three horses costumed as dragons much like that in figure 33, with clawed feet, catlike faces, large sharp teeth, horns, and wings that are clearly suggested at the front shoulders of the horses and slightly protrude above the back.

The imperial dragon—that is, the dragon image that became associated with the emperor and all things surrounding that august personage—is called in the Western tradition a drake, a reptilian dragon without wings. Although often shown without wings, Chinese dragons, by virtue of magical powers, could fly, but this was a rare accomplishment for the Western drakes.

A portrait from the Tang dynasty (626–649) pictures on Emperor Tai-tsung's court robe two drakelike snake-bodied, clawed, and sharp-toothed blue dragons. A vase from the reign of Chia Ching (1532–1455) is decorated with a serpentine, clawed dragon swimming in the ocean, while a sculpture from the same era illustrates the saurian body, claws, vestigial wings, scales, large head, and teeth of the classic world-dragon.

On the "100 Boys" jacket of Empress Xiao Jing, a contemporary of Queen Elizabeth I of England, we see a yellow imperial dragon with a large snakelike body, four clawed feet, and large teeth. In a portrait of Emperor Kanxi of the Ching dynasty, several dragons are depicted. All are four-legged, clawed, and scaled, with horns, "feeler whiskers," and a large mouth full of teeth. Similar types of dragons are delineated on a wine jar from the Ming dynasty of the early sixteenth century, imperial portraits of the Ching dynasty (1736–1795), and a lacquered brush pot from the Wan-li period (1573–1620). In fact, thousands of such images have graced the arts of China for many centuries, and in every case the pictures, sculptures, and reliefs present the basic dragon: a clawed and toothed, reptilian, and flight-capable beast. Though the cultural/artistic styles of Chinese culture influence the manner in which the dragon is represented, the basic creature is clearly visible.

The Eastern dragon's generally good behavior, often contraposed to its Western counterpart's reputation for evil, is explainable as a difference not in type but rather of perception. The classical Eastern dragon was usually described after it had become identified with the emperor—the good, the kind, the benevolent—while the Western dragon, though like the Eastern dragon becoming benevolent in time, was usually described before it became a symbol of state and therefore "under control."

It has been said that Eastern dragons lose toes as they travel east. The imperial dragon of China has five toes, whereas the dragons of Korea and Indonesia generally possess four toes, and the Japanese dragon, three. Japanese dragon myths have borrowed much from China and Korea but also show their own local evolution. The Japanese word *tatsu* is equivalent to the Chinese *lung*. As in Europe and China, dragons in Japan manifest in a number of types. The *sui riu* produces red rain, and the *ri riu* can see prey a hundred miles away. (Emphasis on sharp eyesight is very common among world dragon motifs.) The bright red *ka riu* is only six or seven feet in length, while the *han riu* is a striped creature that can grow up to forty feet.

The dragon motif is pervasive in Japanese art because of a belief about the nature of dragons. In Japanese lore, a dragon gives birth to nine babies, each having a different major attribute. One type likes to carry heavy loads, so the legs of tables are often carved to represent dragon feet. Dragons adorn cups and bowls, since another is fond of drinking. One dragon enjoys bloodshed; therefore swords and sword accoutrements carry dragon images. Pagodas and temples display dragons because one is partial to steep and dangerous locations. Another loves music, another reading, another gongs, and so on; and in each case the dragon's image appropriately decorates the pertinent artifact.

From the *Nihon-gi,* a history of Japan compiled in A.D. 720, we learn that the blood that dripped from the sword of the hero-god Izanagi after he decapitated the fire god became three gods: Kura–okami, Kura–yama-tsumi, and Kura–mitsu-ha. "*Kura-okami* is a dragon- or snake-god who controls rain and snow, and has Shinto temples in all provinces . . . *Kura-okami* means 'the dragon god of the valleys' . . . *Kura-yama-sumi,* is trans-lated 'Lord of the Dark Mountains,' and 'Mountain Snake' . . . *Kura-mitsu-ha* is 'Dark-Water Snake' or 'Valley Water Snake.' " (Macken-zie 1994, 354).

The Japanese *hai-riyo,* or "dragon bird," is a creature with the head and feet of a dragon and the wings and body of a large bird (fig. 35). A number of "dragon birds" manifest themselves in Japan. Near Kyoto, locals claim that a scaled, serpentlike white dragon lives in the center of a lake called Ukisima. Every fifty years it takes the form of *o-gon-cho,* a golden-plumed bird, and rises out of the lake to sing its terrible song—a song more like that of a howling wolf than a song bird. When the song of the *o-gon-cho* is heard, the people know that a season of sickness is upon them. The *o-gon-cho* was last heard to sing in April 1834; famine and dis-ease spread over the local area several months later.

The Japanese also tell the story of an eleventh-century samurai named Tawara Toda who encountered a large, hideous snakelike creature on a bridge one night as he returned home from a party. He did not dis-turb the creature but rather walked calmly past. Later, a beautiful young woman appeared and told him that she was the dragon princess he had seen. After he helped her defeat a giant centipede, she took him to the bottom of a lake, where he met her father, a dragon king, and received a number of magical gifts.

Whereas Chinese dragons usually lived in wells, rivers, and lakes (though there also was a sea dragon), Japanese dragons are very heavily

FIGURE 35: THE JAPANESE *HAI-RIYO,* OR "DRAGON BIRD," IS A CREATURE WITH THE HEAD AND FEET OF A DRAGON AND THE WINGS AND BODY OF A LARGE BIRD.

depicted as sea creatures. The Koshi dragon killed by Susa-no-ow was such a creature, as is the famous contemporary fire-breathing Japanese cinema monster, Godzilla. The "Dragon's Court" is located on the bottom of the sea near the Ryu Ku Islands, which run south from the main islands of Japan. Here lives Ryu-jin, the "Luminous Being," the Japanese sea dragon king, also referred to in Japanese as "Sea Lord" or "Sea Snake." The relationship between dragons and jewels or precious stones is found here in the belief that Ryu-jin controls the tides with his magical "tide jewels," which are sometimes described as pearls.

Donald Mackenzie in *Myths of China and Japan* (1994) writes, "In addition there are horse-dragons, snake-dragons, cow-dragons, toad-dragons, dog-dragons, fish-dragons & etc., in China and Japan. Indeed, all hairy, feathered, and scaled animals are more or less asociated with what may be called the 'Orthodox Dragon'" (47).

The Ainu, the aborigines of Japan, venerate the bear as a major cultural symbol. In traditional times, the Ainu would capture a bear cub in the spring and keep it as a village pet until the following year, when it would be sacrificed in an important religious ritual. The Ainu associated bears and dragons, believing that the bear goddess was the wife of the dragon god. The *Nihon-gi* describes a "bear-dragon" that stretched almost fifty feet in length.

Regarding dragon beliefs of the Chukchi peoples of Siberia, Waldemar Bogoras, author of the definitive work on the Chukchi (1904), comments:

> I mentioned the celestial worm, which is described with the features of a boa-constrictor. . . . Another "giant worm" lives in the sea. It is so strong that it can kill a whale by squeezing it between its coils. A third great Worm also figures in the tales. It is owned by a *ke'le* (nature spirit) and sent by him to drive back the captive maidens who fled from his house. Its tail is fastened in the sleeping-room of the *ke'le,* but its body is so long that its head can overtake the fugitives and run them back. (327)

Many Siberian tribes, including the Chukchi, tell of the "giant fish," or the "giant pike." Unnaturally large, these fishlike creatures live in the

FIGURE 36: THIS DRAGON IMAGE COMES FROM THE LOLO, AN ABORIGINAL POPULATION OF WESTERN CHINA.

deepest lakes. Those who have seen them report that the distance between their eyes measures the length of a boat paddle. With their strong jaws and ferocious teeth, they can snap a boat in half with one bite (fig. 36).

Mackenzie (1994) writes, "In various countries certain fish were regarded as forms of the shape-changing dragon. The Gaelic dragon sometimes appeared as the salmon, and a migratory fish was in Egypt associated with Osiris and his 'mother' " (59).

On the southern periphery of Asia, the Vietnamese have the *long-ma,* or "dragon horse." Their traditions describe the scales of their dragons as fishlike and say that dragons are ancient relatives of the fish that have evolved the ability to fly.

In the Wayang, or "shadow theater," mythology of Java, the king of the dragons, Anantaboga, "Serpent King," lives in his underground lair. Malay Raja Naga, "King of the Serpents," however, lives in the Pusat Tasik, the "Navel of the Oceans," the deepest part of the sea.

The primal dragon image of the giant feathered saurian is evoked in the Indonesian folktale "The Magic Crocodile," when the hero meets the monster for the first time (Terada 1994, 135): "He turned around and nearly fainted from shock and fright. A huge crocodile was walking slowly toward him. It was so enormous that Towjatuwa could not estimate its length. Nor was its appearance like anything he had seen before. Between the scales on its back were feathers of the cassowary bird, giving it a frightful appearance."

In the two-thousand-year old Indian *Rig-Veda,* the god-hero Indra slays the "Dragon of the Clouds," Vrtra, by shooting thunderbolts. This ancient dragon, whose name means "obstruction," was believed to hold the rain in his stomach. When he was slain, the rains fell. Lightning and thunderstorms thus are neatly explained for the peoples of ancient India. The key factor, however, is that Vrtra is a giant flying reptile associated with water—a dragon. Concerning the *nagas* of India, British anthropologist Grafton Elliot Smith (1919) wrote, "The Nagas are depicted in three forms: common snakes guarding jewels; human beings with four snakes in their necks; and winged sea-dragons, the upper part of the body human, but with a horned, ox-like head, the lower part of the body that of a coiling dragon. Here we find a link between the snake of ancient

India and the four legged Chinese dragon" (136). In Tibet *nagas* are shown with the upper body of a human and the lower body of a snake with horns and wings.

At about the time the Sumerian Empire fell, the ancestors of the Hittites migrated out of southern Russia into the Anatolian highlands of modern-day Turkey. In time, from their capital at Hattusa, they spread their influence from the Aegean to the Tigris-Euphrates, north to the Black Sea, and south to the plains of Syria.

Several Hittite myths have been pieced together from broken clay tablets found at ruins. One tells of the storm god's battle with the dragon Illuyanka, a giant serpent with feathered crests, horns, and the ability to spit fire. The dragon was finally destroyed when it was lured from its cavern home with the promise of a banquet for its children and itself. At the party the storm god inebriated the dragon with wine and then killed it.

Heinz Mode (1973) comments, "Thus these few ancient Mesopotamian examples already exhibit some of the basic components of later dragons. Snake, lion, eagle, and scorpion contribute the shapes, and some unidentified animal the horns" (37).

At about the same time that the Hittite Empire was crumbling, the Hebrew peoples were developing their religious concepts and mythologies. As noted in the introduction, dragon references appear throughout the Bible. Daniel, according to the biblical Apocrypha, killed a dragon in Babylon in the temple of Bel, and one of the great dragons of world literature was the mighty Leviathan. This creature and its archenemy, Behemoth, were created, the Bible records, on the fifth day of creation, with Leviathan's purpose being the rule of the world's oceans. The tale concluded that on the Day of Judgment, Leviathan and Behemoth would fight and kill each other, and the righteous of the earth would feast on the Leviathan's flesh. The Book of Job (41:5–25) described Leviathan as a multiheaded sea dragon with huge teeth, hundreds of incandescent eyes, scales, and fiery breath. Its coils could circle the earth, and when it moved, the oceans boiled.

Georgess McHargue, in *The Beasts of Never* (1988), quotes a Hebrew commentator who, in A.D. 1035, wrote an expanded version of the Book of Job:

> Where was thou in the day when I formed the dragon? His food is in
> the sea and his dwelling is in the air; his eyes flash fire; . . . there pours
> forth from him flames as though he were a whirling column of dust;
> his belly burns and his breath flames forth in hot coals like unto rocks;
> it is as though the clash of his teeth were sounds of thunder and the
> glance of his eyes were the flashing of lighting; armies pass him by
> while he is lying; nothing terrifies him. (17)

The Hebrew root word for dragon is *t-n-n,* or *tanniym,* which is generally translated as "dragon" in the Bible, though sometimes as "whale." It
connotes enormous size and immense length.

In the fifth century B.C., the Greek traveler Herodotus wrote of the
winged serpents of Arabia, noting that they came in a number of colors,
enjoyed the trees that produced frankincense, and migrated into Egypt
each spring, where they engaged in epic battle with the Egyptian ibises.

The Phoenicians' dragon, the *agathos daimon,* was imagined as an
invisible winged serpent with a long heart-shaped tongue. Interestingly,
this dragon was believed to be a benign guardian spirit, perhaps a com-
ment on the Phoenician's relatively complex level of political organization at the time they accepted the existence of the *agathos daimon.*

In the Old Testament, when Moses set out to attack an army of
Ethiopians who had invaded Egypt, he took with him baskets of ibises to
fight the flying snakes that could accompany the invaders (fig. 37). It was
generally believed that each spring winged serpents would leave Africa
and encounter their enemies, the ibises, in a deep canyon on the Egyptian border where the ibises would destroy most of the winged serpents.
Cicero, a Roman writer, noted that the exterminating service of the ibis
was necessary because the bite of the winged serpents was known to
cause disease.

Egyptian legends told of snake-necked lions, an image found in
Egypt from earliest times, as well as flying horned snakes, a motif appearing in later Egyptian culture. In one tale Isis was pursued by a dragon
while trying to protect her son. In addition, the dragon-serpent Seth-heh
fought for Ra during his nightly passage through the land of darkness.

Dragons also lived in the abyss along the coast of Ethiopia. Reputed
to reach thirty feet in length, they possessed either two or four wings and

FIGURE 37: A MULTIAPPENDAGED FLYING-SERPENT IMAGE FROM THE SIEN MOUNTAINS OF CHINA. DEPICTED IN THE *SHAN-HAI-KING*.

were particularly skilled at killing elephants. When hunting in Africa was poor, they wove themselves into a raft and floated into Arabia to hunt.

The "magic stone" motif, found in dragons all over the globe, exists here. The ingredients for such a "stone," which could ensure riches and long life, were said to come from the Ethiopian dragon's head. The local twist on the tale alleged that the materials for making the stone could only be taken from a living dragon. To that end, a special potion could be brewed from local herbs that, if one could convince the dragon to drink, would anesthetize the beast long enough to remove the magic stone materials from its head.

In New Zealand, the bishop of Wellington told of a dragon that resided in freshwater lakes, spouted water like a whale, and had a head and teeth that resembled those of a giant crocodile. The native peoples of Australia boast of two types of dragons. The Rainbow Serpent, it is said, lives in deep pools, from which it emerges from time to time to form the rainbow. Through its association with and control of water, it causes storm and flood if angered. It poses a danger to childbearing women, and if they pollute his pools while menstruating or pregnant, the great serpent's rage will be experienced by all. In Australia's Northern Territory, it is called *galeru, ungur, wonunger, worombi, wonambi, wollunqua, yurlunggur, julunggul, langal,* and *muit.* In Queensland, it is known as *yero* and *taipan,* and in southeastern Australia it is *mindi* and *karia.*

We are acquainted with the Australian *bunyip* through myths relating to the Dream Time, or sacred mythic times, of the interior peoples. A young boy sought a gift for his lover, and after a long search he found a strange little animal with a finned tail splashing and playing in a water hole. About the size of a large dog, the little creature was covered in shining scales. Its dragonlike face with glowing eyes resembled that of a bulldog, with a wide mouth full of sharp teeth.

The true nature of the gift became apparent when a short time later the creature's mother appeared to rescue it from its human kidnappers. "Mother" was a giant lizardlike dragon with flashing scales and many fanglike teeth. Its roar sounded like thunder, and soon the people saw the rivers and lakes rising to flood stage and inundating the land. In further revenge the *bunyip* turned those who had taken her baby into a flock of black swans (Shuker 1995, 64–65).

In Hawaii in 1850, the native people living in the vicinity of present-day Pearl Harbor informed the missionaries that the drastic fall in oyster production was due to a *mo-o,* a saurian sea monster who had moved the local oyster bed to another location.

The *mo-o,* also *mo-ko,* are a classification of the *'aumakua,* the ancestral gods. Varieties of *mo-o* abound, but most have some association with water, rain, and storms. Hawaiian images of *mo-o* detail a large, often black, heavy-bodied reptile with four legs, scales, fanglike teeth, and a length of about thirty feet. Emphasizing that the Polynesian dragon does not seem to be derivable from images in nature, Reverend Bloxam, the English naval chaplain on board the *Blonde* in the early 1800s, discussed the difficulty in understanding the Hawaiians' description of the *mo-o,* since they "had nothing of the shape of serpents or large reptiles in their islands" (cited in Mackenzie 1994, 69).

In the eastern regions of modern-day Ecuador and Peru live the horticultural Shuara. A people famous for their incessant raiding and head-taking (and shrinking!), they are particularly interested in rituals that guide boys to manhood and full warrior status. When a Shuara boy reaches the age of puberty, his relatives honor him with a feast to initiate his incorporation into adult male Shuara society. Following the feast, he is given a hallucinogenic drink called *maikoa,* which is made from the bush *Datura arborea.* Isolated, usually in the vicinity of a waterfall, an area sacred among the Shuara, the boy experiences frightful visions of various spirits that to become a man he is directed to overcome. Rafael Karsten (1990) writes, "The most important of these spirits are the so-called *arumtama* ("the old ones") which are in their nature the souls of the ancestors. These appear in all sorts of terrible shapes, as *tigers* (Jaguars), *eagles, giant snakes* [emphasis added], and other wild animals, or reveal their presence in stupendous phenomena of nature, in the lightning, in the rainbow, in meteors, etc." (304–5).

Far to the north of the Shuara, the Aztec employed not only the winged serpent-dragon but also the double-headed serpent motif and conventional saurian dragon images. Around 500 B.C.–A.D. 900 among the Maya of the Yucatan Peninsula, Kulkulkan, the plumed serpent, was an important deity. The Maya incorporated feline features into the Kulkulcan plumed serpent image, as well as into images of Chac, the

Mayan rain god. Chac is shown with a serpent's body in the Dresden Maya Codex and sometimes with wings, horns, and crests in other Mayan media. The double-headed serpent motif also appears among the Maya on Stela N at Copan, Honduras, as well as on the east side of Altar O at Copan.

Specialists in Olmec culture, the most ancient high culture of Mesoamerica, believe that the plumed serpent cult of the later Toltecs, Mayans, and Aztecs evolved from an earlier Olmec jaguar cult. Various forms of Olmec art carry creatures with the combined elements of the raptor, serpent, and jaguar—the dragon complex (Fig. 38, 39). The phrase "jaguar serpent" comes from the ancient "Song to Tlaloc" from Teotihuacan. The "jaguar serpent" was later incorporated with the image of the owl among the Toltec, thus completing the typical dragon complex image.

Non-state-level societies in classic Mesoamerica demonstrated an awareness of dragons. The hunting and gathering Huicholes of northern Mexico considered plumed serpents to be the cause of rain and storms. And at the time of Spanish contact on the coast of Yucatan, village fishermen spoke of Itzamna, the serpent god of the East, and of Itzam-kabain, a whale-like creature with alligator feet, teeth, and claws.

On the lower Missouri River, not far from the Mississippi River cliff where the Piasa dragon (noted in the introduction) can be seen to this day, a Cheyenne tale is set that explains why traditional Cheyenne always made an offering of food or tobacco when crossing a deep body of water. In ancient times two men were hunting along the river when they came upon several very large eggs. One man ate some of the eggs, while his partner refrained. Slowly, in the days following, the man who had consumed the eggs transformed into a giant feathered serpent. In time, bidding his friend good-bye, he disappeared into the Missouri River, a tongue of flame rising from the swirl where he submerged (Marriotte and Rachlin 1974, 71–72). The Cheyenne also told of the *minio,* the horned, hairy water spirits who sometimes caught careless individuals as they walked near their abodes in deep pools—and dragged them to a watery death.

On the Northwest coast of the United States, the Haida and the Kwakiutl Indians feared the Sisiutl, sometimes depicted as a double-

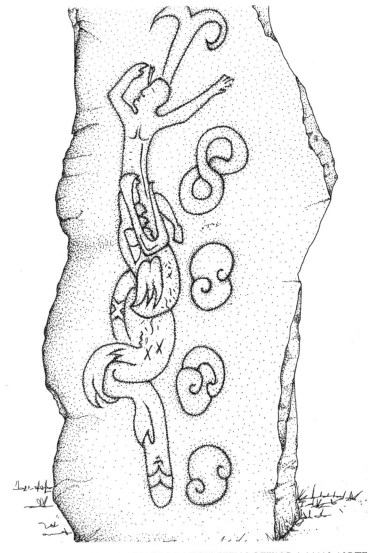

FIGURE 38:IMAGE OF AN OLMEC DRAGON SWALLOWING A MAN. NOTE THE LARGE TEETH, WINGS, SERPENT BODY, AND ACCOMPANYING IMAGES THAT ARE VERY REMINISCENT OF THE CLOUD AND WAVE EMBLEMS FROM CHINESE DRAWINGS OF DRAGONS.

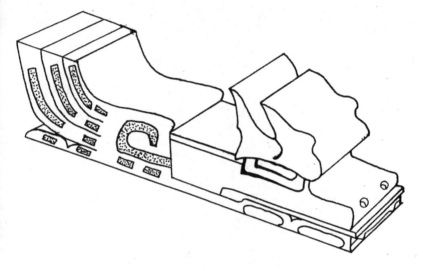

FIGURE 39: A HIGHLY STYLIZED OLMEC DRAGON IMAGE.

headed serpent and sometimes with four clawed feet and a snakelike tail, and of a size big enough to swallow a man. Among the Kwakiutl, the Sisi-utl was honored in the winter ceremonies where it was presented as a monster that could bring death simply by its touch, assume the shape of a fish at will, and grant powers to those it favored.

A painted screen from the Nootka of Vancouver Island depicts the dragon complex in a grouping of a raptor (Thunderbird), serpent (Lightning Serpent), and carnivore (Wolf). From the Tlingit Indians of Alaska, a carved image of a dragon-headed boat carries seven spirits to the spirit world.

In the era of the Southern Ceremonial Complex (circa 1450–1650) among groups ancestral to the historic Cherokee (as well as the Creeks, Choctaws, Chickasaws, and Natchez), many images of men with antlers, wings, talons, snakelike tails, and breechcloths with a spotted pattern, perhaps representing the scales of serpents, were etched on shell, bone, wood, and ceramics. The classic *uktena* and the Water Cougar are also found in the art motifs of the Southern Ceremonial Complex.

In conclusion, it is interesting to note that what I refer to as the dragon complex is the title of famed art historian Miguel Covarrubias's 1967 work on the Indian art of Alaska, Canada, and the United States: *The Eagle, the Jaguar, and the Serpent*.

BIBLIOGRAPHY

Agras, S., D. Sylvester, and D. Oliveau. 1969. "The Epidemiology of Common Fears and Phobias." *Comprehensive Psychiatry* 10: 151–56.

Alterman, L., Gerald A. Doyle, and M. Kay Izard, eds. 1993. *Creatures of the Dark: The Nocturnal Prosimians.* New York: Plenum Press.

Altmann, Stuart A. 1967. *Social Communication among Primates.* Chicago: University of Chicago Press.

Bailey, Theodore N. 1993. *The African Leopard.* New York: Columbia University Press.

Barash, David P. 1977. *Sociobiology and Behavior.* New York: Elsevier.

Barker, W. H., and Cecilea Sinclair. 1917. *West African Folk-Tales.* London: George G. Harrap.

Barnouw, Victor. 1985. *Culture and Personality.* Homewood, Ill.: Dorsey Press.

Bascom, William R. 1994. *African Dilemma Tales.* Chicago: Aldine.

Base, Graeme. 1996. *The Discovery of Dragons.* New York: Harry N. Abrams.

Baskin, Hosie, and Leonard Baskin. 1985. *A Book of Dragons.* New York: Alfred A. Knopf.

Bastien, Joseph W. 1978. *Mountain of the Condor.* Prospect Heights, Ill.: Waveland Press.

Berger, I. R., and R. J. Clarke. 1995. "Eagle Involvement in Accumulation of the Taung Child Fauna." *Journal of Human Evolution* 29, no. 3: 275–99.

Blest, A. D. 1957. "Function of Eyespot Patterns in the Lepidoptera." *Behaviour* 11: 210–54.

Boaz, Noel T., and Alan J. Almquist. 1997. *Biological Anthropology: A Synthetic Approach to Human Evolution.* Englewood Cliffs, N.J.: Prentice Hall.

Bogoras, Waldemar. 1904. *The Chuckchee.* Leiden: E. J. Brill.

Borges, Jorge Luis. 1969. *The Book of Imaginary Beings.* New York: Avon.

Bramblett, Claud A. 1976. *Patterns of Primate Behavior.* Mt. View, Calif.: Mayfield.

Brown, Donald E. 1991. *Human Universals.* New York: McGraw-Hill.

Brown, Leslie. 1971. *African Birds of Prey.* Boston: Houghton Mifflin.

Brown, Robert W. 1954. "Mass Phenomena." In *Handbook of Social Psychology,* vol. 2, edited by Gardner Lindzey, 833–73. Reading, Mass.: Addison-Wesley.

Calhoun, Craig, Donald Light, and Suzanne Keller. 1989. *Sociology.* 6th ed. New York: McGraw-Hill.

Capek, Abe. 1962. *Chinese Stone-Pictures.* London: Spring Books.

Charbonneau-Lassay, Louis. 1991. *The Bestiary of Christ.* Translated by D. M. Dooling. New York: Parabola.

Chiarelli, A. B. and R. S. Corruccini, eds. 1981. *Primate Behavior and Sociobiology.* New York: Springer-Verlag.

Christensen, Erwin O. 1955. *Primitive Art.* New York: Bonanza Books.

Coe, Ralph T. 1976. *Sacred Circles: Two Thousand Years of North American Indian Art.* Kansas City, Mo.: Helen G. Bonfils Charitable Trust.

Conroy, Glenn C. 1990. *Primate Evolution.* New York: W. W. Norton.

Cook, Roger. 1974. *The Tree of Life.* New York: Avon.

Covarrubias, Miguel. 1967. *The Eagle, the Jaguar, and the Serpent.* New York: Alfred A. Knopf.

Cunningham, Scott. 1994. *Hawaiian Religion and Magic.* St. Paul, Minn.: Llewellyn.

Davies, Nigel. 1977. *The Toltec.* Norman: University of Oklahoma Press.

Dickinson, Peter. 1979. *The Flight of Dragons.* New York: Harper & Row.

Ditmars, Raymond. 1931. *Snakes of the World.* New York: Macmillan.

Droscher, Vitus B. 1970. *The Friendly Beast.* New York: Harper & Row.

Eggan, Dorothy. 1974. "Hopi Dreams in Cultural Perspective." In *Culture and Personality,* edited by Robert A. Levine, Chicago: Aldine. 265–84.

Eibl-Eibesfeldt, Irenaus. 1989. *Human Ethology.* New York: Aldine de Gruyer.

Eliade, Mircea. 1958. *Patterns in Comparative Religion.* Cleveland: World Publishing Company.

Eliot, Alexander, ed. 1976. *Myth.* New York: McGraw-Hill.

Elliot-Smith, Grafton. 1919. *The Evolution of the Dragon.* London: University Press.

Ember, Carol R., and Melvin Ember. 1993. *Anthropology.* Englewood Cliffs, N.J.: Prentice Hall.

Epstein, Perle. 1973. *Monsters: Their Histories, Homes, and Habits.* Garden City, N.Y.: Doubleday.

Evans, Jonathan Duane. 1984. "A Semiotic of the Old English Dragon." In *Dissertation Abstracts International* (DAI) Ann Arbor, MI. Vol. 45, no. 6.

Everett, Michael. 1976. *Birds of Prey.* New York: G. P. Putnam's Sons.

Farley, John E. 1998. *Sociology.* 4th ed. Upper Saddle River, N. J.: Prentice Hall.

Feder, Kenneth L., and Michael Alan Park. 1993. *Human Antiquity.* Mountain View, Calif.: Mayfield.

Fontenrose, Joseph. 1959. *Python: A Study of Delphic Myth and Its Origins.* Berkeley and Los Angeles: University of California Press.

Franklin, Stan. 1995. *Artificial Minds.* Cambridge, Mass.: MIT Press.

Frazer, James George. 1961. *The New Golden Bough.* New York: Doubleday.

Furst, Peter T., and Jill L. Furst. 1982. *North American Indian Art.* New York: Rizzoli.

Gardner, Howard. 1985. *The Mind's New Science: A History of the Cognitive Revolution.* New York: Basic Books.

Gelder, M. G., and I. M. Marks. 1966. "Severe Agoraphobia: A Controlled Prospective Trial of Behavior Therapy." *British Journal of Psychiatry* 112: 309–19.

Gillette, D. D., and M. G. Lockley. 1989. *Dinosaur Tracks and Traces.* Cambridge, England: Cambridge University Press.

Goldstein, A. J., and D. L. Chambless. 1987. "A Re-analysis of Agoraphobia." *Behavior Therapy* 9: 59.

Goode, Erich. 1992. *Collective Behavior.* New York: Harcourt Brace Jovanovich.

Gould, Charles. 1886. *Mythical Monsters.* London: W. H. Allen & Co.

Gould, Steven S. 1977. *Ontogeny and Phylogeny.* Cambridge, Mass: Harvard University Press.

Graziosi, Paolo. 1960. *Paleolithic Art.* London: Faber and Faber.

Griffin, Donald R. 1984. *Animal Thinking.* Cambridge, Mass.: Harvard University Press.

Haslerud, G. M. 1938. "The Effect of Movement of Stimulus Objects upon Avoidance Reactions in Chimpanzees." *Journal of Comparative Psychology* 25: 507–28.

Haviland, William A. 1994. *Human Evolution and Prehistory.* New York: Harcourt Brace.

Hayes, L. Newton. 1923. *The Chinese Dragon.* Shanghai: Commercial Press.

Heuvelmans, Bernard. 1986. *In the Wake of the Sea-Serpent.* New York: Hill and Wang.

Hinde, R. A. 1974. *Biological Bases of Human Social Behavior.* New York: McGraw-Hill.

Hoebel, E. Adamson. 1960. *The Cheyennes: Indians of the Great Plains.* New York: Holt, Rinehart and Winston.

Hoffman, Walter James. 1897. *The Graphic Art of the Eskimos.* New York: AMS Press.

Holliday, Trenton. 1998. Personal communication. Department of Anthropology, Tulane University.

Holowell, A. Irving. 1955. *Culture and Experience.* Philadelphia: University of Pennsylvania Press.

Hudson, Charles. 1976. *The Southeastern Indians.* Memphis: University of Tennessee Press.

——— 1987. "The Southeast Woodlands." In *Native American Religions: North America,* edited by Lawrence E. Sullivan. New York: Macmillan.

Huneker, James. 1915. *Ivory Apes and Peacocks.* New York: Charles Scribner's Sons.

Hutchinson, H. N. 1892. *Extinct Monsters: A Popular Account of Some of the Larger Forms of Ancient Animal Life.* New York: D. Appleton & Company.

Inverarity, Robert Bruce. 1971. *Art of the Northwest Coast Indians.* Berkeley and Los Angeles: University of California Press.

Jersild, A. T,. and F. B. Holmes. 1935. "Children's Fears." In *Child Development Monograph,* no. 20.

Jochelson, Waldemara. 1908. *The Koryak.* Leiden: E. J. Brill.

———. 1926. *The Yukaghir and The Yukaghirized Tungus.* Leiden: E. J. Brill.

Jolly, Alison. 1966. *Lemur Behavior: A Madagascar Field Study.* Chicago: University of Chicago Press.

———. "Thinking Like a Vervet." *Science* 251:574.

Kappeler, Peter M., and Jorg U. Ganzhorn. 1993. *Lemur Social Systems and Their Ecological Basis.* New York: Plenum Press.

Karsten, Rafael. 1990. "Blood Revenge and War among the Jibaro Indians of Eastern Ecuador." In *Law and Warfare,* edited by Paul Bohannan. Austin: University of Texas Press.

Kavanagh, Michael. 1983. *A Complete Guide to Monkeys, Apes and Other Primates.* London: Jonathan Cape.

Kendall, Diana. 1998. *Sociology in Our Times: The Essentials.* Belmont, Calif.: Wadsworth Publishing Company.

Kitchener, Andrew. 1991. *The Natural History of the Wild Cats.* New York: Comstock.

Knipe, Rita. 1989. *The Water of Life: A Jungian Journey through Hawaiian Myth.* Honolulu: University of Hawaii Press.

Konner, Melvin. 1982. *The Tangled Wing.* New York: Harper & Row.

Lancaster, Jane Beckman. 1975. *Primate Behavior and the Emergence of Human Culture.* New York: Holt, Rinehart and Winston.

Laporte, Leo F. 1978. *Evolution and the Fossil Record.* San Francisco: W. H. Freeman and Company.

Laughlin, Charles D., J. McManus, and Eugene d'Aquili. 1992. *Brain, Symbol and Experience: Toward a Neurophenomenology of Human Consciousness.* New York: Columbia University Press.

Levinson, David. 1996. *Religion: A Cross-Cultural Encyclopedia.* New York: Oxford University Press.

Macedonia, Joseph M. 1993. "Adaptation and Phylogenetic Constraints in the Antipredator Behavior of Ringtailed and Ruffed Lemurs." In *Lemur Social Systems and their Ecological Basis.* New York: Plenum Press.

Mackenzie, Donald A. 1994. *Myths of China and Japan.* New York: Gramercy Books.

Maglio, Vincent J., and H. B. S. Cooke. 1978. *Evolution of African Mammals.* Cambridge, Mass.: Harvard University Press.

Marks, Isaac M. 1969. *Fears and Phobias.* New York: Academic Press.

————. 1987. *Fears, Phobias, and Rituals* New York: Oxford University Press.

Marriott, Alice, and Carol K. Rachlin. 1974. *American Indian Mythology.* New York: Mentor Books.

Martin, R.D. 1990. *Primate Origins and Evolution: A Phylogenetic Reconstruction.* Princeton, N.J.: Princeton University Press.

Mavissakalian, Matig. 1981. *Phobia.* New York: Guilford Press.

McGee, Jon R. 1990. *Life, Ritual, and Religion among the Lacandon Maya.* Belmont, Calif.: Wadsworth.

McGee, Jon R., and Richard L. Warms. 1996. *Anthropological Theory: An Introductory History.* Mountain View, Calif.: Mayfield.

McHargue, Georgess. 1988. *The Beasts of Never.* New York: Delacorte.

Medalia, Nehum Z., and Otto N. Larson. 1958. "Diffusion and Belief in a Collective Delusion: The Seattle Windshield Pitting Epidemic." *American Sociological Review* 23:221–32.

Melville, Joy. 1977. *Phobias and Obsessions.* New York: Coward, McCann & Geoghegan.

Miller, George A. 1956a. "The Magical Number Seven, Plus or Minus Two: Some Limits on Our Capacity for Preocessing Information." *Psychological Review* 63, no. 2:81–96.

————. 1956b. "Information and Memory." *Scientific American*, August, 42–46.

Mode, Heinz. 1973. *Fabulous Beasts and Demons.* London: Phaidon.

Morris, Desmond. 1967. *The Naked Ape.* New York: Dell.

Morris, R., and D. Morris. 1965. *Men and Snakes.* London: Hutchinson.

Morris, Henry M. 1993. *Dragons in Paradise.* El Cajon, Calif.: Institute for Creation Research.

Moseley, Michael E. 1992. *The Incas and Their Ancestors.* London: Thames and Hudson.

Neihardt, John G. 1972. *Black Elk Speaks: Being the Life Story of a Holy Man of the Oglala Sioux.* New York: Washington Square Press.

Nesse, Randolph M. 1991. "What Good Is Feeling Bad? The Evolutionary Benefits of Psychic Pain," *Sciences*, November/December, 30–37.

Newman, Paul. 1980. *The Hill of The Dragon: An Enquiry into the Nature of Dragon Legends.* Totowa, N.J.: Rowman & Littlefield.

Nigg, Joe. 1995. *Wonder Beasts: Tales and Lore of the Phoenix, the Griffin the Unicorn, and the Dragon.* Englewood, Colo.: Libraries Unlimited.

Parker, Sue Taylor, and Kathleen Rita Gibson. 1979. "A Developmental Model of the Evolution of Language and Intelligence in Early Hominids." *Behavioral and Brain Sciences* 2, no. 3 (September).

Passes, David. 1993. *Dragons: Truth, Myth and Legend.* New York: Western Publishing.

Peters-Golden, Holly. 1994. *Culture Sketches: Case Studies in Anthropology.* New

York: McGraw-Hill.

Pfeiffer, John E. 1982. *The Creative Explosion*. Ithaca, N.Y.: Cornell University Press.

Pliny the Elder. *Natural History*. Vol. 3. Translated by H. Rackham. Cambridge, Mass.: Harvard University Press.

Poignant, Roslyn. 1967. *Oceanic Mythology*. New York: Paul Manlyn.

Powers, William K. 1987. "Lakota." In *Native American Religions: North America*, edited by Lawrence E. Sullivan. New York: Macmillan.

Preiss, Byron, John Betancourt, and Keith R. A. DeCandido, eds. 1995. *The Ultimate Dragon*. New York: Dell.

Rachman, S. *Phobias*. 1988. Springfield, Ill.: Charles C. Thomas.

Ray, Dorothy Jean. 1977. *Eskimo Art: Tradition and Innovation in North Alaska*. Seattle: University of Washington Press.

Russell, Findlay E. 1980. *Snake Venom Poisoning*. Philadelphia: J. B. Lippincott.

Russell, P. A. 1979. "Fear-Evoking Stimuli." In *Fear in Animals and Man*, edited by W. Sluckin, 86–126. New York: Van Nostrand.

Sagan, Carl. 1977. *The Dragons of Eden: Speculations on The Evolution of Human Intelligence*. New York: Ballantine.

Seidelman, Harold, and James Turner. 1994. *The Inuit Imagination*. London: Thames and Hudson.

Seigel, Richard A., and Joseph T. Collins. 1993. *Snakes*. New York: McGraw-Hill.

Seligmann, M. E. P. 1971. "Phobias and Preparedness." In *Biological Boundaries of Learning*, edited by Seligmann and Hager.

Service, Elman R. 1978. *Profiles in Ethnology*. 3d ed. New York: Harper Collins.

Seyfarth, Robert M., Dorothy L. Cheney, and Peter Marler. 1980. "Monkey Response to Three Different Alarm Calls: Evidence of Predator Classification and Semantic Communication." *Science* 210:801–3.

Shuker, Karl. 1995. *Dragons: A Natural History*. New York: McGraw-Hill.

Simon, Herbert A. 1974. "How Big Is a Chunk?" *Science* 183: 482–88.

Sluckin, W. 1979. *Fear in Animals and Man*. New York: Van Nostrand Reinhold.

Smith, S. M. 1975. "Innate Recognition of Coral Snakes Pattern by a Possible Avian Predator." *Science* 187:759–60.

Spawls, Stephen, and Bill Branch. 1995. *The Dangerous Snakes of Africa*. Sanibel Island, Fla: Ralph Curtis.

Spinar, Zdenek. 1972. *Life before Man*. New York: American Heritage.

St. John, Donald P. 1989. "Iroquois." In *Native American Religions: North America,* edited by Lawrence E. Sullivan. New York: Macmillan.

Struhsaker, T. T. 1967. "Auditory Communication among Vervet Monkeys." In *Social Communication among Primates*, edited by S. A. Altman. Chicago: University of Chicago Press.

Sullivan, Lawrence E., ed. 1989. *Native American Religions: North America*. New

York: Macmillan.

Sweeney, James B. 1972. *A Pictorial History of Sea Monsters and Other Dangerous Marine Life*. New York: Crown.

Taylor, David. 1990. *The Kingdom of Animals*. New York: Starlight Editions.

Terada, Alice M. 1994. *The Magic Crocodile and Other Folktales from Indonesia*. Honolulu: University of Hawaii Press.

Time-Life Books. *Life before Man*. New York: Time-Life. 1972.

Tinbergen, N. 1959. *The Study of Instinct*. Oxford: Clarendon Press.

Townsend, Richard F. 1992. *The Aztecs*. London: Thames and Hudson.

Turi, Johan. 1966. *Turi's Book of Lappland*. Costernout, the Netherlands: Anthropological Publications.

van den Berghe, Pierre L. 1997. *Man in Society*. New York: Elsevier.

Visser, Willem de. 1969. *The Dragon in China and Japan*. Wiebaden: M. Sandig.

Wallace, Anthony F. C. 1970. *Culture and Personality*. New York: Random House.

Wallace, Ronald L. 1983. *Those Who Have Vanished*. Homewood, Ill. Dorsey Press.

Washburn, S. L., and Ruth Moore. 1980. *Ape into Human: A Study of Human Evolution*. Boston: Little, Brown and Company.

Wauchope, Robert. 1962. *Lost Tribes and Sunken Continents*. Chicago: University of Chicago Press.

Westervelt, W. D. 1987. *Myth and Legends of Hawaii*. Honolulu: Mutual Publishing Company.

Whiteley, Peter M. 1987. "The Southwest." In *Native American Religions: North America*, edited by Lawrence E. Sullivan. New York: Macmillan.

Wilson, Edward O. 1975. *Sociobiology: The New Synthesis*. Cambridge, Mass.: Belknap Press, Harvard University Press.

———. 1978. *On Human Nature*. Cambridge, Mass.: Harvard University Press.

Wolpoff, M. H. 1980. *Paleoanthropology*. New York: Alfred A. Knopf.

Zallinger, Peter. 1986. *Dinosaurs and Other Archosaurs*. New York: Random House.

Zorn, Elayne L. 1998. Personal communication. University of Central Florida, Orlando.

INDEX